An Introduction to
Latin Prose Composition

An Introduction to Latin Prose Composition

Milena Minkova

An Introduction to
Latin Prose Composition

by Milena Minkova

Published by:
WPC Classics
P.O. Box 9779
London SW19 7QA
United Kingdom

Email: sales@wpcpress.com
Fax: (+44) 20 8944 0825

ISBN: 1898855 43 9

Produced in the UK
Printed in Hungary

WPC Classics is an imprint of the Wimbledon Publishing Company
P.O. Box 9779, London SW19 7QA

Qui Latine scribit scripta antiquiorum
melius intellegit....

Prooemium

Cum nonnullos abhinc annos munus institutionis artis Latine scribendi apud Pontificiam studiorum universitatem Gregorianam restaurandae suscepissem, praelectionibus dilucidis opus fuit quibus alumni ad Latinitatem colendam allicerentur. Vitari oportuit ne res grammatica cognoscendi solum causa tractaretur neu nimium de sermone ornando usu simpliciter Latine componendi neglecto dissereretur. Itaque pedetemptim haec conscripsi quae nunc praesenti libello Anglice reddita continentur. Qui libellus decem capitibus totum unum constituens quomodo sententiae Latinae exarentur iisque exaratis quomodo scriptum fiat gradatim docet. Propositum mihi erat summam rerum brevissime limpidiusque exponere. In hoc opere arduo, cum praesertim aliud esset praelectiones aliud enchiridion scribere, studii Latinitatis socii me magnopere adiuverunt. Ipso initio Professor Tuomo Pekkanen Finnus omnia et singula benigne ac salubriter castigavit. Item Professor Michael de Albrecht Heidelbergensis animum corroborare necnon de via rationeque agendi humane monere non destitit. Dein Profestrix Iana O'Neill ex Collegio Davidsoniensi in Carolina Septentrionali libellum pro humanitate sua perlegit et nonnulla mutanda proposuit. Denique Professor David Morgan ex Carolina Meridiana omnia minutissime percensuit, sine cuius auxilio eximiaque benignitate liber numquam exstitisset. Manuscriptum iam domui editoriae traditum Professor Ioannes Traupman emendavit. Quibus omnibus professoribus, collegis, amicis ex imo corde summas gratias ago atque habeo. Omnia tamen quae in libello parum emendata manent mihi tantum sunt attribuenda.

Porro gratiae mihi sunt referendae Patri Sebastiano Grasso S.I. Scholae superioris litterarum Latinarum apud Pontificiam studiorum universitatem Gregorianam directori qui me quondam ascivit ut in eadem Schola artem Latine scribendi docerem.

Praecepta atque exercitationes quae hoc libello comprehenduntur alumnis meis profuerunt. Si cui lectori quoque usui fuerint, haud frustra lucubrasse mihi videbor.

Milena Minkova

Scribebam Romae et in Carolina Septentrionali, ab A.D. MCMXCVII usque ad A.D. MM.

Contents

Contents

Contents

Chapter I
Simple Sentence

A simple sentence can convey different types of messages: using a simple sentence we can state a fact, either affirmatively or negatively; refer to something which could be or could not be; ask a question; express doubt or deliberation; command or forbid certain things; exhort; make a wish; temporarily concede something which, in fact, we do not accept; and, finally, we can exclaim. There are four sentence types: declarative, interrogative, imperative, and exclamatory. The declarative sentence is usually an affirmative or a negative statement of a fact, a statement of possibility, or a counterfactual statement. The interrogative sentence asks questions and denotes doubt or deliberation. The imperative sentence makes commands, prohibitions, exhortations, wishes, or concessions. The exclamatory sentence type conveys its message with emphasis. It is on account of different illocutionary forces, i.e., the different intents on the part of the speaker as revealed from the context, that each of the four types of sentence can generate more than declarative, interrogative, directive, and exclamatory sentences.

This chapter reviews ways of expressing the following:

1. Statement of fact.
2. Negative statement of fact.
3. Statement of possibility.
4. Counterfactual statement.
5. Question.
6. Doubt or deliberation.
7. Command.
8. Prohibition.
9. Exhortation.
10. Wish.
11. Concession.
12. Exclamation.

1. Statement of fact

a) To state a fact, we simply use a declarative sentence and one of the six tenses of the indicative.

- The present tense expresses an action which happens in the present (corresponds to the present simple or to the present progressive in English).

*Linguam Latinam **disco**.*
I study Latin (or I'm studying Latin).

The present is used also for proverbs and statements of general validity.

*Fortes fortuna **adiuvat**.*
Fortune helps the courageous.

Using the present, we often report past actions in a particularly lively manner (the historical present).

*Clamores **tolluntur**. Populus **concurrit**. Turba **fit** frequens.*
Shouts were raised. People ran together. A huge crowd gathered.

- The imperfect tense expresses a repeated, habitual, or continuing action in the past. It is used for conditions and states, which by definition are continuous. In narration, the imperfect is generally used for description and background information.

*Rex filiam **habebat** pulcherrimam.*
The king had a very beautiful daughter. (a continuing action)

*Amicum cottidie **adibam**.*
I used to visit my friend every day. (a habitual action)

- The perfect tense has two distinct uses. One is to express a definite, non-continuous action that happened at a certain moment in the past. (In this use, it is usually equivalent to the simple English past tense.) In narration, the perfect is used for the actions occurring in sequence that form the basic plot line.

Veni, vidi, vici.
I came, I saw, I conquered.

The other use of the perfect is to express the present result of a past action. (In this use, it is usually equivalent to the English present perfect tense, or sometimes to the present passive which emphasizes the existing circumstances.)

Exegi *monumentum aere perennius.*
I have built a monument more enduring than bronze.

Gallia omnis **divisa est** *in partes tres.*
The whole of Gaul is divided into three parts.

- The pluperfect tense describes an action in the past which had happened before another action in the past.

Fuerat *inimicus. Postea amicus est factus.*
He had been an enemy. Afterwards he became a friend.

- The future tense expresses an action which will happen in the future.

Erunt *primi novissimi.*
The last will be first.

- The future perfect tense expresses an action which will have happened before another action in the future. It occurs most often in subordinate clauses of sentences whose main clause has the simple future tense. (In English a present tense is generally used where Latin uses the future perfect.)

*Cum **cenavero**, ambulabo.*
After I eat dinner, I will go for a walk.

b) The present infinitive, called in this case the historical infinitive, is sometimes used for past action. The historical infinitive gives a sense of vividness to dramatic moments in a narration.

*Igni perterriti omnes **fugere**. **Complere** vias. **Sterni** per agros.*
Everybody was running, frightened by the fire. People were crowding the streets. They were throwing themselves to the ground.

c) The negative rhetorical question states a fact in a lively way. It may be accompanied by *enim*.

Quis** enim stultitiam tuam **non videt?
Everybody sees your stupidity.

2. Negative statement of fact

a) A negative statement of fact is made by using negative adverbs or negative pronouns.

• Negative adverbs:

non (usually negating the verb or the entire clause);
haud (negating a single word, in most cases an adjective or an adverb);
minime, haudquaquam, nequaquam (expressing a categorical negative statement);

ne ... quidem (expressing "not even", and applying the negation to the word between *ne* and *quidem*);
numquam (negative for time);
nusquam (negative for place);
nullo modo (negative for manner).

Non possum plura scribere.
I cannot write any more.

Haud mirabile est.
There is nothing to wonder about.

Hoc ad te minime pertinet.
This is none of your business at all.

Haudquaquam semper fortuna est secunda.
Fortune is by no means always favorable.

Nequaquam gaudeo.
I am not glad at all.

Ne auro quidem vir honestus corrumpitur.
The man of integrity is not bribed even with gold.

Tempus elapsum numquam revertitur.
Time, once gone, never comes back.

Fratrem nusquam invenio.
I cannot find my brother anywhere.

Nullo modo id possum credere.
I cannot believe it in any way.

The negative adverb is a part of the verbs *nescio, nolo, nequeo*.

Pisces ire nequeunt.
Fish cannot walk.

- Negative pronouns and adjectives:

nemo (a negative pronoun for persons);
nullus (a negative adjective);
neuter (a negative pronoun for the negation of two persons or things);
nihil (a negative pronoun for things).

Nemo sine vitio est.
No one is without fault.

Nullus deorum metus, nullum iusiurandum, nulla religio ei fuit.
He did not have any fear of gods, any faith, any piety.

Neuter consulum bello abesse potuit.
Neither of the consuls could be absent from the war.

Nihil sub sole novum.
There is nothing new under the sun.

N.B. Two negations render the statement positive:

non nemo - someone;
nemo ... non - everyone;
non nulli - some people;
nulli ... non - all people;
non nihil - something;
nihil ... non - all things;
non numquam - sometimes;
numquam ... non - always;
non nusquam - somewhere;
nusquam ... non - everywhere.

Non est placandi spes mihi nulla dei.
I have some hope in appeasing the deity.

Nemo non didicisse mavult quam discere.
Everyone prefers to have learned than to be learning.

In Latin two negations always make a positive statement. That is why, if the force of the statement is to be negative, only one word in the statement can be negative - normally the one whose negativity is to receive the greatest emphasis. When there are other concepts in the sentence that are in a sense caught up in an overall negative sweep, they will be expressed by certain indefinite pronouns or adverbs that tend to correlate in Latin with negative words, much as in English "ever" correlates with "never," and "any" with "none." In this way, *nemo* corresponds to *quisquam, nullus* to *ullus, nihil* to *quicquam* or *ulla res, numquam* to *umquam,* and *nusquam* to *usquam.*

Numquam ulla civitas Româ potentior fuit.
<u>Never</u> was any city more powerful than Rome.

Nulla civitas umquam Româ potentior fuit.
<u>No</u> city has ever been more powerful than Rome.

Numquam is emphasized in the first sentence and *nulla* in the second.

Iustitia numquam nocet cuiquam.
Never does justice do harm to anyone.

Numquam quicquam stultius audivi.
Never have I heard anything more stupid.

Nemo usquam doctior invenitur.
No one more learned is to be found anywhere.

b) The positive rhetorical question makes a negative statement in a lively way. It may be accompanied by *enim.*

Quid enim est turpius?
There is nothing more shameful than that.

3. Statement of possibility

a) A statement of possibility in the present and the future is made with the present subjunctive (especially for actions envisaged as continuing), or, more rarely, with the perfect subjunctive (especially if the action is envisaged as being quickly accomplished). The negation used is *non*.

Verba tua sine ulla dubitatione semper **confirmem**.
I would always confirm your words without any hesitation.

Aliquis **dixerit**.
Someone might say.

b) The imperfect subjunctive, usually addressing an imaginary second person, expresses a pure hypothesis for the past.

Ista **non crederes**.
One would not have believed those things.

c) Possibility can of course also be expressed by the various tenses of *possum* and an infinitive.

Aliquis **dicere potest**. = *Aliquis dixerit.*

d) Possibility can also be denoted by the indicative, if accompanied, for example, by the adverb *fortasse*.

Fortasse *quispiam* **quaeret**.
Someone might ask.

4. Counterfactual statement

a) We make a statement contrary to a fact in the present with the imperfect subjunctive, and statement contrary to a fact in the past with the pluperfect subjunctive. However, these types of subjunctives are rarely used in a simple sentence. They usually occur in the principal clause of a conditional sentence. The negation used is *non*.

*Sine te **non viverem**.*
I would not live without you. (In fact I do live with you.)

*Sine tuo auxilio **servatus non essem**.*
I would not have been rescued without your help. (In fact I was rescued with your help.)

b) A counterfactual statement for the past could be expressed by a past tense of *possum* and an infinitive.

*Sine tuo auxilio **servari non potui**. = Sine tuo auxilio servatus non essem.*

5. Question

a) We may ask questions using interrogative particles, interrogative pronouns, and interrogative adverbs.

• Interrogative particles:

-ne - is used for a question expressing no assumption about whether the answer will be negative or affirmative; the particle *-ne* is attached to the word the question focuses on;
nonne - is used for a question that anticipates a positive answer;
num - is used for a question that anticipates a negative answer.

*Vivit**ne** pater?* -
<u>Is</u> your father alive (or not)?

Vivit. Sane. Ita. Etiam. Certe. Vero. Sane quidem.
Yes.

Non vivit. Non vero. Non ita. Minime.
No.

*Pater**ne** vivit? - Ipse vivit.*
Is your <u>father</u> (as opposed to the mother or to someone else) alive?
- He is alive.

***Nonne** meministi? - Memini.*
You do remember, don't you? - Yes, I do.

***Num** latine scit? - Minime.*
He doesn't know Latin, does he? - No, he doesn't.

We will also consider here disjunctive questions, which are introduced by:

utrum ... an**, **-ne ...an - when there is a choice between two different answers;
utrum (-ne) ... annon (or ***necne*** if the question is indirect) - when the choice is between "yes" and "no."

*Postrema syllaba **utrum** brevis est **an** longa?*
Is the last syllable short or is it long?

*Est**ne** postrema syllaba brevis **an** longa?*
Is the last syllable short or is it long?

***Utrum** postrema syllaba brevis est **annon**?*
Is the last syllable short or not?

●   Interrogative pronouns and adjectives:

quis, quid - interrogative pronoun, without a distinctive form for the feminine;
qui, quae, quod - interrogative adjective;
quisnam, quidnam - interrogative pronoun for a question expressing wonder or emotion "*just who? who in the world?*";
quinam, quaenam, quodnam - interrogative adjective for a question with wonder or emotion "*just which?*";
uter, utra, utrum - asks who or which of two persons or two things;
qualis, quale - asks about kind or quality;
quantus, a, um - asks about size;
quot - (indeclinable) asks about cardinal numerals;
quotus, a, um - asks about ordinal numerals;
quoteni, ae, a - asks about distributive numerals;
cuias, cuiatis - asks about origin;
quanti - asks about price.

Quid prodest?
What good is it?

Quis hic loquitur?
Who is talking here?

Qui vir hic loquitur?
Which man is talking here?

Quae mulier hic loquitur?
Which woman is talking here?

Quisnam me miserum adiuvabit?
Who could it be that will help poor me?

Uter *consulum occisus est?*
Which of the two consuls has been killed?

Qualis *orator est ille?*
What kind of speaker is he?

Quantam *fidem habes?*
How much faith do you have?

Quot *estis?*
How many are you?

Quota *hora est?*
What time is it?

Per **quotenas** *horas singulis diebus linguam Latinam discis?*
How many hours do you study Latin every day?

Cuiates *estis?*
Where do you come from?

Quanti *panem emisti?*
How much did you pay for the bread?

- Interrogative adverbs:

ubi - *where?*
quo - *to what place? whither?*
unde - *from what place? whence?*
quando - *when?*
quamdiu - *how long?*
quousque - *until when? how long?*
quotiens - *how many times? how often?*
quomodo; *ut* - *how?*
cur; *quare* - *why?*

Ubi patera nunc est?
Where is the dish now?

Quo vadis?
Where are you going?

Unde iste amor tam improvisus venit?
Where does this unexpected love come from?

Quando te videbo?
When will I see you?

Quamdiu apud nos manebis?
How long are you going to stay with us?

Quousque abuteris patientia nostra?
How long will you try our patience?

Quotiens auxilium petivisti?
How many times did you ask for help?

Quomodo dormivisti?
How did you sleep?

Ut vales?
How are you?

Cur irasceris?
Why are you getting angry?

Quare me vocas?
Why do you call me?

● A note on the mood of the question:

The indicative in a question implies that one is asking about a real fact. See many examples above.

The present or perfect subjunctive in a question can be used in asking about a possibility.

Veniasne *mecum?*
Would you come with me? (If I go, and I may actually do so.)

The imperfect or pluperfect subjunctive in the question may indicate that what we are asking for is contrary to a fact in the present or in the past.

Veniresne *mecum?*
Would you come with me? (If I were going, but I am not.)

Venissesne *mecum?*
Would you have come with me? (If I had gone, but I did not.)

b) Sometimes even a declarative sentence may ask a question with the indicative.

*Certe patrem tuum non **occidisti.***
Did you kill your father?

6. Doubt or deliberation

We express doubt or deliberation with a deliberative question. The tenses and moods that are used are the present subjunctive if the doubt or the deliberation is related to the present or the future, and the imperfect subjunctive if the doubt or the deliberation is related to the past. The negative used is *non*.

*Quo me nunc **vertam**? Undique custodior.*
Where to turn now? Guards are watching me from everywhere.

*Quid tunc **agerem**?*
What was I to do at that moment?

*Egone illum **non fleam**?*
Should I not cry over him?

7. Command

a) We usually command with the present imperative, or, more rarely, with the future imperative (which is used especially in legal texts). The present imperative suggests that the command is to be executed immediately, while the future imperative reserves execution of the commanded action for the future. The present subjunctive provides a milder alternative to the imperative; it does not so much command as advise or suggest. Moreover, since present imperative forms exist only for the second person, in order to make a third person command, we use the present subjunctive, or, more rarely, the future imperative.

***Da** mi basia mille!*
Give me a thousand kisses!

***Ignoscito** semper alteri, numquam tibi!*
Always forgive your fellow man, never yourself!

*Saepe stilum **vertas**!*
Turn the stylus often (to erase what you have written)!

***Audiatur** et altera pars!*
Hear the other side as well!

*Salus populi suprema lex **esto**!*
The welfare of the nation should be the highest law!

b) An interrogative sentence may also imply a command.

***Quin** taces?*
Shut up!

c) The command sometimes can be expressed even by the indicative.

*Tu hoc **facies**.*
Just do it!

8. Prohibition

We prohibit by using *ne* and usually the perfect subjunctive. To prohibit in a milder way, one may use *noli, nolite* with the present infinitive. This type of prohibition is possible only for the second person. *Ne* and the future imperative is a negative precept.
The expressions *fac ne*, *vide ne*, *cave ne* or simply *cave*, all of them with the subjunctive, are also used in prohibition.

***Ne** vos mortem **timueritis**!*
You all do not dare to be afraid of death!

***Noli turbare** circulos meos!*
Don't disturb my figures! (words of Archimedes to a soldier from the conquering army)

*Hominem mortuum in urbe **ne sepelito**!*
Do not bury a dead person in the city!

***Cave festines**!*
Don't rush!

9. Exhortation

a) Exhortation is advice, encouragement, or admonition. It is used mainly in the first person plural and is expressed by the present subjunctive. *Ne* is used in negative exhortations.

Amemus *patriam!*
Let us love our fatherland!

Ne difficilia **optemus***!*
Let us not desire what is difficult!

The mild third person command is a kind of exhortation as well.

Suum quisque **noscat** *ingenium!*
Everyone should know his own character!

b) An exhortation may also be expressed by *debeo* and an infinitive or by the passive periphrastic conjugation. In that case, it partly points to our duty to do something.

Patriam **amare debemus**. *= Patria nobis* **est amanda**. *= Amemus patriam!*

10. Wish

To express a wish for something possible in the present or the future, we use the present subjunctive. To express a wish for something impossible in the present, we use the imperfect subjunctive. To express a wish for something impossible for the past, we use the pluperfect subjunctive. To express a wish for an event in the past, without knowing whether it was realized or not, we use the perfect subjunctive. The subjunctive is often accompanied by *utinam*. The negation used is *ne*.

17

*Di omnia bona tibi **dent**!*
May the gods give you all good things!

*Illud **utinam ne** vere **scriberem**!*
Would that I were not really writing it! (But unfortunately I am really writing it.)

***Utinam** nostri **vicissent**!*
If only our people had won! (But unfortunately they lost.)

***Utinam** litteras meas **acceperis**!*
Hopefully you received my letter! (You may have received it or not.)

11. Concession

Sometimes, for the sake of argument or for rhetorical reasons, we admit temporarily what in reality we do not believe. Such a concession is made with the present subjunctive if it refers to the present, and with the perfect subjunctive if it refers to the past. The negative is *ne*.

Sit fur!
Let us suppose (for the sake of argument) that he is a thief! (But in fact he is not and we will demonstrate that.)

Ne sit fur!
Let us suppose that he is not a thief! (But in fact he is and we will demonstrate that.)

*Malus civis **fuerit**!*
Let us suppose that he has been a bad citizen! (But in fact he has been a good citizen and we will demonstrate that.)

12. Exclamation

An exclamation may take the following forms:

a) An exclamation may take the form of a normal sentence containing a verb and the word *quam* modifying an adjective, adverb, or verb.

Quam *multa fecisti!*
How many things you have done!

Quam *laudari cupiunt!*
How much they desire to be praised!

b) An exclamation may take the form of a sentence containing no verb, but consisting rather of a noun in the accusative, expressing the object of the exclamation. Such an exclamation is often accompanied by the interjection *o*.

Me miserum*!*
Poor me!

O, fallacem *hominum* **spem***!*
Oh, deceitful human hope!

c) An exclamation may take the form of various interjections followed by nouns in the appropriate cases. These too are sentences without a verb.

ecce; **en** - with the nominative: to show or indicate something;
ei; **vae** - with the dative: to express pain or compassion;
bene - with the accusative: in drinking to one's health;
pro(h) - with the nominative: to express pain or surprise.

Ecce *homo!*
Here is the man!

Vae *victis!*
Woe to the defeated!

Bene *nos!*
I drink to our health!

Pro *dolor!*
It is a pity!

d) An exclamation may take the form of an interjection without any other word. These of course are also sentences without a verb.

•   Interjections strictly speaking:

O! - joy, surprise, desire, pain, indignation;
Vah! - surprise, joy, anger;
Atat! Attat! Atatatae! Attatatate! Atatte! Atattate! - joy, pain, surprise, fear, admonition;
Babae! Papae! - joy and surprise;
Eia! Heia! - joy and pleasant surprise;
Euhoe! Euoe! Evoe! - joy;
Io! - joy;
Euge! - joy, approval, admiration;
Ah! A! - pain, sadness;
Heu! Eheu! - pain;
Hem! - surprise;
Heus! - drawing attention;
Ne! - affirmation.

•   Interjections derived from other words:

Utinam!
Would to heaven!

Bene!
Good!

Male!
Bad!

Recte!
Right!

Nefas!
Terrible!

Nefandum!
Terrible!

Pulchre!
Great!

Malum!
The devil!

Praeclare!
Excellent!

Indignum!
Shameful!

Apage!
Away!

Age! Agite! Agedum!
Come on!

Edepol! Pol!
Truly! Upon my word! Honestly!

Mecastor!
Truly! Upon my word! Honestly!

Hercule! Hercle! Mehercules!
Truly! Upon my word! Honestly! Good gracious!

Medius fidius!
Truly! Upon my word! Honestly!

e) An exclamation may take the form of an accusative and infinitive construction:

Te nunc, mea Terentia, sic vexari!
My Terentia, you are so distressed now!

f) Finally, a question with *ut* and the subjunctive can be exclamatory as well.

Tu ut umquam te corrigas?
You will never change! (Cicero's words to Catiline)

Chapter II
Coordinate Connections

A coordinate connection is one that connects either two independent sentences or two clauses in the same compound sentence.

Esurio. **Itaque** *cibum capio.*
I am hungry. So I eat.

Panem comedo **et** *vinum bibo.*
I eat bread and drink wine.

The main coordinate connections are: copulative (affirmative and negative), disjunctive, adversative, causal, consecutive, temporal and local, topic-changing, result in case of an unfulfilled condition, revision of a previous statement, and stronger negative.

1. Copulative connection

a) *Affirmative copulative connection*

- We use the following conjunctions in order to establish an affirmative copulative connection:

et - for a common connection;
-que - for a tight connection;
atque (*ac*) - for a specifying connection;
necnon - for an additive or increasing connection.

Divide et impera!
Divide and conquer!

Te precor oroque.
I beg and entreat you.

Imperium superatum est atque depressum.
The empire has been overcome and subdued.

Scientia adiuvat necnon ornat.
Science helps and embellishes as well.

- **Asyndeton**, namely the omission of conjunctions, is also a kind of a copulative connection.

Veni, vidi, vici.
I came, I saw, I conquered.

- Some copulative conjunctions are used not only between the clauses of a compound sentence, but also to connect independent sentences. Such copulative conjunctions are:

etiam (first position) - expressing intensification;
quoque (second position) - expressing addition.

*Omnia vobis enarravi. **Etiam** unam rem vos orare velim.*
I told you everything. In addition, I want to ask you something.

*In meam caedem inimici coniuraverunt. Tu **quoque**, Brute, coniuravisti.*
The enemies formed a plot to slay me. You too, Brutus, participated in the plot.

- A **relative pronoun** at the beginning of the sentence can also serve as a copulative connection to the preceding sentence.

Legati venerunt ad petendam pacem. **Quibus** *Caesar sic respondit.*
Ambassadors came to ask for peace. And Caesar answered them in
the following way.

b) *Negative copulative conjunctions*

- **neque, nec**

Opinionibus vulgi rapimur in errorem **nec** *vera cernimus.*
Popular opinion drags us into errors, and we cannot discern the truth.

- *Ne ... quidem* connects independent clauses. It applies the
  negation with an emphasis on the word in between: *not even.*

Pacem perdidimus. **Ne** *obsidibus* **quidem** *datis eam obtinere
potuimus.*
We lost the peace. We could not keep it even by giving hostages.

c) *Correlative copulative conjunctions*

et ...et ... - both ... and ...;
neque ... neque ...; nec ... nec ... - neither ... nor ...;
cum ... tum ... - *both ... and especially ...;*
non solum ... sed etiam ...; *non modo ... verum etiam ...* - *not only
... but also ....*

Et domino satis et furi nimium.
Both enough for the owner and too much for the thief.

Neque amat quemquam neque amatur ab ullo.
He neither loves anybody, nor is loved by anybody.

Haec sententia visa est cum vera, tum honesta.
This opinion seemed both true and honorable.

Non solum *doceri,* **sed etiam** *delectari discipuli volunt.*
The students want not only to be taught, but also to be entertained.

2. Disjunctive connection

a) Ordinary disjunctive conjunctions

aut - connection between two incompatible elements;
vel - connection between two elements from which one can choose.

Vinceris **aut** *vincis.*
You will either be defeated or you will win.

Ipse veniam **vel** *fratrem mittam.*
I will come myself or I will send my brother.

b) Correlative disjunctive conjunctions

aut ... aut ... - connection between two incompatible elements;
vel ... vel ... - connection between two elements from which one can choose;
sive (seu) ... sive (seu) ... - used especially when we are not sure which of two concepts is the right one.

Aut *dic* **aut** *abi!*
Either speak or go away!

Vel ipse faciam **vel** *alium rogabo.*
I will either make it myself or ask someone else (as I please).

Haec vocalis **sive** *producta est* **sive** *correpta.*
This vowel can be either long or short.

3. Adversative connection

• The adversative connection can connect either two clauses of a compound sentence or two independent clauses. The adversative conjunctions are the following:

sed (first position) - the most common adversative conjunction;
verum (first position) - indicates a strong contradistinction;
vero (second position) - indicates a weak contradistinction;
autem (second position) - indicates a weak contradistinction;
at (first position) - introduces a very different thought;
tamen (first or second position) - less strong conjunction.

*Amicus Plato, **sed** magis amica veritas.*
Plato is dear to me, but the truth is dearer.

*Haec non a natura, **verum** a magistro didici.*
I have learned these things not from nature, but from a teacher.

*Tres copiarum partes hostes flumen transduxerunt, quarta **vero** citra flumen mansit.*
The enemy transported three fourths of their army across the river; the last fourth, however, remained on this side of the river.

*Rumoribus mecum pugnas, ego **autem** a te rationes requiro.*
You fight against me with popular opinions. I, however, ask you for arguments.

*Vix credibile est. **At** sic res se habent.*
It seems hardly credible. Nevertheless, such is the situation.

*Naturam expelles furca, **tamen** usque recurret.*
You can force nature out with a pitchfork, but it will always come back.

- The **relative pronoun** at the beginning of the independent clause can also establish an adversative connection with the preceding sentence.

Themistocles a patre exheredatus est. **Quae** *contumelia non fregit eum sed erexit.*
Themistocles was disinherited by his father. However, this affront did not break down his spirit, but emboldened him.

4. Causal connection

The causal connection is used between two independent sentences when the latter gives the cause of the former one or explains in some way the information given in the former one. The causal conjunctions have a similar meaning and are the following:

nam (first position);
enim (after one or more words);
namque (usually first position);
etenim (first position).

Amici non solum inter se diligunt, sed etiam verentur. **Nam** *sine verecundia vera amicitia esse non potest.*
Friends not only love but also respect each other. For there cannot be true friendship without respect.

Mihi omne tempus est meos ad libros vacuum. Numquam **enim** *illi sunt occupati.*
I always have time for my books. In fact, they are never busy either.

Felix mihi videor. **Namque** *omnia necessaria fortuna mihi dedit.*
I consider myself fortunate. For fortune has given me everything I need.

Verus es amicus. **Etenim** *amicitiam tuam comprobasti.*
You are a true friend. You have indeed given a proof of your friendship.

5. Consecutive connection

- The consecutive connection is normally used between two independent sentences, the latter of which is in some way a consequence of the former. The consecutive conjunctions are the following:

ergo (first or second position) - expresses a logical consequence;
igitur (always preceded by one or more words) - expresses a logical consequence;
itaque (first position) - indicates a fact as a consequence;
proinde - expresses a desired consequence.

Cogito, **ergo** *sum.*
I think, therefore I exist.

Homines perfecti non sunt. Falli **igitur** *possunt.*
Human beings are not perfect. And so they can be deceived.

Nemo liber ausus est mortuum sepelire. **Itaque** *a servis sepultus est.*
No freeman dared to bury the dead man. And so he was buried by slaves.

Eos ferre non possum. **Proinde** *aut exeant aut quiescant.*
I cannot stand them. So they should either get out or keep quiet.

- We may also use the conjunctions **ideo, idcirco, propterea, inde, eo** for a consecutive connection.

- The **relative pronoun** at the beginning of the sentence may also establish a consecutive connection to the preceding sentence.

*Multas ad res perutiles Xenophontis libri sunt. **Quos** legite studiose.*
The books of Xenophon are very useful for many things. So read them eagerly.

6. Other coordinate connections

There are also other coordinate connections. They are used mainly to connect independent sentences.

a) *Temporal and local connection*

- These words indicate a coordinate connection of a temporal or local nature:

tum; tunc - then;
deinde; dein; exinde; inde; deinceps; post; postea - afterwards;
subinde - immediately after;
denique, tandem, postremo - at last;
hic - here;
illic; ibi - there;
hinc - from this place, hence;
illinc - from that place, thence;
huc - to this place, hither;
illuc - to that place, thither.

*Signum pugnae est datum. **Tum** milites conclamaverunt.*
A signal to attack was given. Then the soldiers shouted together.

Hostes contra legiones suas instruunt. **Deinde** *utrique imperatores in medium exeunt.*
The enemies organize the legions on their side. Then both generals go into the center.

Romae per biduum commorabimur. **Hinc** *Neapolim proficiscemur.*
We will stop off in Rome for two days. From here we will leave for Naples.

- These correlative temporal conjunctions are used within a compound sentence:

modo ... modo ... - sometimes ... at other times;
tum ... tum ... - at one moment ... at another.

Modo *loquebatur,* **modo** *tacebat.*
Now he was speaking, now was silent.

Tum *currebat,* **tum** *consistebat.*
At one moment he would run, at another he would stop.

b) Topic-changing connection

ceterum - otherwise, besides, yet, but.
porro - furthermore, moreover.

Argentum accepi. **Ceterum** *nil aliud curavi.*
I received the money. Otherwise nothing mattered to me.

Patrem et matrem honores. **Porro** *Deum ne neglexeris.*
Respect your father and your mother. Moreover, do not disregard God.

c) *Result in case of an unfulfilled condition*

alioquin - otherwise.

Exitu felici gaudebo. **Alioquin** *ipse me consolabor.*
I will be glad to be successful. Otherwise I will console myself.

d) *Revision of a previous statement*

immo - to the contrary; in fact; or I should say (correcting, expanding upon, or going beyond what has just been said).

Etiam mihi nonnulla sunt vitia. **Immo** *plurima.*
I too have some defects. In fact, I have a great many defects.

e) *Stronger negative connection*

nedum - still less, much less, not to speak of (usually followed by the subjunctive).

Ne ditissimus quidem rex hanc terram emere potest. **Nedum** *tu possis.*
Not even the richest king can buy this land - much less could you.

Chapter III
Subordination

In order to communicate a complex message, we need to use subordination. There are a number of types of subordination from which we can choose.

Depending on how complex our message will be and how many levels of subordination we want to introduce, we may use subordinate clauses of the first, second, third, or higher degrees.

Petivi auxilium, (main clause)
quod mihi necessarium erat, (subordinate 1st degree)
ut hostes vincerem. (subordinate 2nd degree)
I asked help, which was necessary in order to overcome the enemy.

Depending on the form we want to adopt, we may construct explicit or implicit subordinate clauses. The explicit clauses have a conjugated verb and are introduced by a connecting word. The implicit clauses, as explained below, do not look like a clause, but like a phrase, since they do not contain a conjugated verb.

Depending on the logical value of what we want to communicate, our subordinate clause may be substantive, adjectival, or adverbial. This is discussed on the following pages.

Subordinate clauses are divided according to form into explicit and implicit subordinate clauses. An explicit subordinate clause contains a conjugated verb; an implicit one does not.

Explicit subordinate clauses are introduced by: 1) conjunctions (the case for most such clauses); 2) relative pronouns or relative adverbs (relative clauses); 3) interrogative pronouns or interrogative adverbs (indirect questions). Explicit subordinate clauses have a finite verb.

When explicit subordinate clauses are constructed with the indicative, the tenses preserve their original meaning (see *I. Simple sentence, 1. Statement of fact*). When they are constructed with the subjunctive, the rule of the sequence of tenses determines the use of the tenses.

In applying the rules of the **sequence of tenses**, we must first distinguish two sorts of sentences: one in which the main clause has a principal tense (present, future or future perfect), and the other in which the main clause has a historical tense (imperfect, perfect or pluperfect). The action expressed in the dependent clause may be contemporaneous with the action in the main clause, it may precede it, or it may follow it.

A contemporaneous action after a principal tense is to be expressed by the present subjunctive, while a contemporaneous action after a historical tense is to be expressed by the imperfect subjunctive.

A preceding action after a principal tense is expressed by the perfect subjunctive, while a preceding action after a historical tense is expressed by the pluperfect subjunctive.

A subsequent action is usually expressed in the same way as a contemporaneous action, the action of the subordinate clause being understood to apply generally to a period of time from that of the principal clause onward.

In the clause *Oro te ut venias,* for instance, the time of *venias* is both contemporaneous with and subsequent to that of *oro*. If we want to emphasize that *venias* applies to a moment in the future, we may use a temporal adverb or another temporal indication, e.g., *Oro te ut cras venias.*

Only in those situations in which the concept of contemporaneity is clearly distinguished from the concept of subsequence, such as interrogative questions and sentences with *non dubito quin*, do we use the present subjunctive of the periphrastic conjugation to express a subsequent action following a main tense, and the imperfect subjunctive of the periphrastic conjugation to express a subsequent action following a historic tense, e.g.,

Interrogo te quid agas. (id est quid agas nunc, hodie) -
Interrogo te quid acturus sis. (id est quid acturus sis cras, in posterum);
Non dubito quin hanc rem curet (hoc ipso temporis momento curat) -
Non dubito quin hanc rem sit curaturus (cras vel futuris temporibus curabit).

See in detail the rules of the sequence of tenses under *Indirect question* in this chapter.

With respect to explicit subordinate clauses and subordinate clauses which are in the second, third, or higher degrees (i.e., embedded in other subordinate clauses), it is also necessary to note the rule of **attraction of mood**. When the main clause has the subjunctive or the infinitive, an expected indicative in the subordinate clause may be changed to subjunctive, e.g., *Ita fit ut quod bonum <u>sit</u>, id etiam honestum sit.* So attraction of mood is sometimes used in subordinate clauses of the second, third, or higher degrees.

<u>**Implicit**</u> subordinate clauses, i.e., subordinate clauses without a conjugated verb, are not introduced by a conjunction, a relative pronoun or adverb, or an interrogative pronoun or adverb. They are of the following types: the accusative and infinitive construction, the participle construction, the ablative absolute, the gerundive construction expressing a purpose, and the supine.

We need also to remember the proper use of the **reflexive pronoun** and the **possessive pronoun** in the third person. This use is the same in both explicit and implicit subordinate clauses. In the main clause, the reflexive pronoun always refers to the subject. In subordinate clauses it may refer either to the subject of the main clause or to the subject of the subordinate clause itself. It refers to the subject of the main clause when the subordinate clause expresses a thought or the will of the subject of the main clause. (This is the case for the accusative with infinitive construction, indirect questions, purpose clauses, and clauses with the objective *ut* after verbs expressing will.) It refers to the subject of the subordinate clause, when the latter indicates an objective fact. (This is the case for result and temporal clauses.) The difference can be observed in the following examples:

*Petitor postulabat ut praemium **sibi** traderetur.*
The candidate asked the prize to be given to him.

*Petitor·ita se egit ut praemium **ei** sit traditum.*
The candidate performed so well that the prize was given to him.

According to their function in the sentence, subordinate clauses may be divided into three groups. For purposes of this classification, each subordinate clause is considered as functioning logically as an element of the main clause: noun, adjective, or adverb.

1. **Substantive** or **complementary** clauses comprise the first group. These clauses have the logical value of a substantive. They function in the main clause as subject of the verb, as direct object, or, rarely, as appositives, and so they necessarily complete the sense of the main clause. That is why they are called substantive or complementary. We use them when, instead of a simple substantive in the main clause, we need to communicate a more complex message.

2. **Adjectival** or **attributive** clauses comprise the second group. These clauses have the logical value of an adjective. They function as an attribute to a noun in the main clause. That is why they are called adjectival or attributive. We use them when, instead of a simple adjective in the main clause, we need to communicate a more complex attribute.

3. **Adverbial** or **circumstantial** clauses comprise the third group.

They have the logical value of an adverb. They function as an adverb that adds some circumstantial meaning to the verb in the main clause. That is why they are called adverbial or circumstantial. We use them when, instead of a simple adverb in the main clause, we need to communicate more complex circumstances.

1. Substantive or complementary clauses

We use substantive clauses when we wish to communicate a more complex message than can be expressed by a simple substantive used as subject, direct object, or appositive. In this case the logical subject, direct object, or appositive consists of an entire clause. The subordinate clause is called **subjective** when it functions as subject of the sentence, **objective** when it functions as direct object, and **epexegetic** when used in apposition with a substantive of the main clause. If the subordinate clause serves as subject or direct object, it is a necessary part of the main clause.

In general, the cases in which we use substantive clauses may be summarized as follows. They are used as an extended direct object after verbs that express what the subject says, thinks, asks, and doubts, what he feels, desires, requests, advises, or commands, what he sees to having done, what he achieves, fears or hinders, what he adds or is silent about, what is good or bad to do or not to do for him. Except for the last notion, which contains an exterior judgment of the subject's action, the verbs which require a substantive clause generally express a thought, a statement, a wish, an endeavor, or a feeling of the subject. If the verb is in the passive voice, a substantive clause which would normally be an extended direct object becomes an extended subject. Substantive clauses are also used as extended subjects after impersonal verbs and impersonal phrases which signify that something happens, is usual, is necessary, is allowed, is good, is bad, or is known.

Finally, substantive clauses are used as extended appositives (quite a rare case) with neuter singular pronouns; in this case, the clauses provide further information about the meaning of the pronouns.

Substantive clauses take the following forms: accusative with infinitive; indirect questions; clauses with the explicative *quod*; clauses with the explicative *ut*; clauses with the objective *ut* (mainly after verbs expressing will); clauses after verbs of fearing; clauses after *non dubito quin* and similar expressions; clauses after verbs of preventing and refusing.

• *Accusative with infinitive*

We use the accusative with infinitive construction as an extended direct object with the following types of verbs:

Verbs of saying (*dico, narro, refero, affirmo, nego, respondeo, scribo,* etc.);

Verbs of believing and perceiving (*puto, credo, intellego, sentio, video, arbitror, credo, scio, nescio, spero,* etc.);

Verbs of will and desire (*volo, nolo, malo, cupio, opto, iubeo,* etc.);

Verbs of emotion (*gaudeo, laetor, miror, doleo, angor, aegre fero,* etc.). These verbs, however, are also constructed with the causal *quod* (see *3. Adverbial or circumstantial clauses, b) How to express a causal circumstance.*)

The accusative with infinitive construction is an extended subject after the verbs listed above when they are used impersonally, and after the following impersonal verbs and phrases:

decet, dedecet, oportet, licet, interest, refert, constat; fama est, bonum est.

The accusative with infinitive construction is an implicit clause. It functions practically as a clause, though it is not introduced by a conjunction. Its subject and any predicate noun are in the accusative, its verb in the infinitive.

The three tenses of the infinitive are used in the accusative with infinitive construction. The present infinitive indicates an action contemporaneous with that of the main clause (after any tense in the main clause). The perfect infinitive indicates an action preceding that of the main clause (after any tense in the main clause). The future infinitive indicates an action following that of the main clause (after any tense in the main clause).

Contemporaneity (the present infinitive)

Puto te errare.
I think that you are making a mistake.
Putavi te errare.
I thought that you were making a mistake.
Puto te in errorem induci.
I think that you are led into making a mistake.
Putavi te in errorem induci.
I thought that you were led into making a mistake.

Precedence (the perfect infinitive)

Puto te erravisse.
I think that you made a mistake.
Putavi te erravisse.
I thought that you had made a mistake.
Puto te in errorem inductum esse.
I think that you were led into making a mistake.
Putavi te in errorem inductum esse.
I thought that you had been led into making a mistake.

Posteriority (the future infinitive)

Puto te erraturum esse.
I think that you will make a mistake.
Putavi te erraturum esse.
I thought that you would make a mistake.

Puto te in errorem inductum iri.
I think that you will be led into making a mistake.
Putavi te in errorem inductum iri.
I thought that you would be led into making a mistake.

*Thales dixit **aquam esse initium** rerum.*
Thales said that water was the beginning of things.

*Spero **te** hoc **esse adepturum**.*
I hope that you will reach this goal.

*Volo **te clementissimum existimari**.*
I want you to be considered a very lenient person.

***Salvum te advenisse** gaudeo.*
I am glad that you arrived safe and sound.

***Oratorem irasci** minime decet.*
It is not at all proper for the orator to be in a rage.

*Fama est **hostes esse peremptos**.*
There is a report that the enemies have been slain.

- ## *Indirect question*

We use indirect questions as extended objects after verbs of asking, investigating, observing, understanding, thinking and similar actions. Indirect questions are introduced by interrogative particles, interrogative pronouns, and interrogative adverbs in the same manner as direct questions. The difference is in the fact that the indirect question is constructed with the subjunctive, which follows the rules of the sequence of tenses. (The present subjunctive of the periphrastic conjugation is used to express posteriority after a principal tense in

the main clause, and the imperfect subjunctive of the periphrastic conjugation is used to express posteriority after a historical tense in the main clause).
Here again are the rules of the sequence of tenses.

Contemporaneity (the present subjunctive or the imperfect subjunctive in indirect question)

Interrogo te quid agas.
I ask you what you are doing.
Interrogavi te quid ageres.
I asked you what you were doing.

Precedence (the perfect subjunctive or the pluperfect subjunctive in indirect question)

Interrogo te quid egeris.
I ask you what you have done.
Interrogavi te quid egisses.
I asked you what you had done.

Posteriority (the present subjunctive of the periphrastic conjugation or the imperfect subjunctive of the periphrastic conjugation in indirect question)

Interrogo te quid acturus sis.
I ask you what you are going to do.
Interrogavi te quid acturus esses.
I asked you what you were going to do.

*Quaeris a me **num** recte faciam.*
You ask me whether I am doing it the right way.

*Pater quaesivit a filio velle**ne** secum proficisci.*
The father asked the son whether he wanted to leave with him.

*Cupio scire **ubi** sis hiematurus.*
I wish to know where you are going to spend the winter.

Indirect questions may also be indirect expressions of doubt or deliberation (see *1. Simple message, 6. Doubt or deliberation*).

***Quid** faciam nescio.*
I do not know what to do.

- ### *Clauses with the explicative quod*

We use clauses with the explicative *quod* as extended direct objects after verbs and phrases such as the following:

bene (male) facio;
addo, mitto, praetereo.

We use clauses with the explicative *quod* as extended subjects after the following verbs and phrases:

bene (male, opportune) accidit (evenit, fit);
additur, accedit;
bonum (molestum, gratum) est.

Clauses with the explicative *quod* are constructed with the indicative.

*Bene mihi evenit **quod** mittor ad mortem.*
It is a good thing for me to be sent to die. (words of Socrates before drinking the hemlock)

*Accessit **quod** etiam pluere incepit.*
To this was added the fact that it started raining.

*Bonum est **quod** ad me venisti.*
It is good that you came to me.

*Bene facis **quod** me adiuvas.*
You do well in helping me.

*Adde **quod** perferri litterae non potuerunt.*
Add the fact that the letter could not be delivered.

Sometimes we use a clause with the explicative *quod* as an extended appositive with a neuter pronoun in the main clause. Such a clause is called epexegetic.

*Hoc praestamus maxime feris **quod** colloquimur inter nos.*
We are superior to the animals especially in that we speak with one another.

• *Clauses with the explicative ut*

We use clauses with the explicative *ut* as extended subjects of the following verbs and phrases:

accidit ut, evenit ut, contingit ut, fit ut, fieri potest ut;
mos est ut, moris est ut, consuetudo est ut.

These clauses are always constructed with the subjunctive, and follow the rules of the sequence of tenses.

*Natura fit **ut** liberi a parentibus amentur.*
It happens naturally that children are loved by their parents.

*Illa nocte accidit **ut** esset luna plena.*
That night there happened to be a full moon.

• *Clauses with the objective ut*

We use clauses with the objective *ut* as extended objects after the following verbs (most of them express will):
Verbs of wishing and demanding (*oro, rogo, peto, volo, flagito, postulo*, etc.);
Verbs of urging (*hortor, moneo, admoneo, suadeo, persuadeo, impero,* etc.);
Verbs of endeavoring (*curo, consulo, facio, operam do*, etc.);
Verbs of achieving (*consequor, impetro, obtineo, adipiscor*, etc.).

If the clause is negative, it is introduced by *ne*.

Clauses with the objective *ut* are constructed with the present subjunctive after a principal tense in the main clause, and with the imperfect subjunctive after a historical tense in the main clause.

*Volo **ut** mihi respondeas.*
I want you to answer me.

*Cura **ut** valeas.*
Take care to be in good health.

*Videant consules **ne** quid res publica detrimenti capiat.*
The consuls should see to it that the state suffer no harm.

*Monui **ut** tibi consuleres.*
I recommended that you look after your own interests.

*Adepti estis **ne** hostes metueretis.*
You managed not to fear the enemies.

After the forms *fac, facite, velim, vide*, we can use the subjunctive without a conjunction.

*Velim mihi **scribas** aut potius **scriptites**.*
I would like that you write me or rather that you write me often.

• *Clauses after verbs of fearing*

The expanded direct object after verbs of fearing (*timeo, metuo, vereor,* etc.) takes the form of a clause introduced by *ne* if the subject fears that something undesirable may happen, and *ne non* (or *ut*) if the subject fears that something desirable may not happen. These clauses are normally constructed with the present subjunctive after a principal tense in the main clause, and with the imperfect subjunctive after a historical tense. However, if the fear pertains to a time period preceding that of the main verb, the clause is constructed with the perfect subjunctive after a principal tense and with the pluperfect subjunctive after a historical one.

*Timeo **ne** hostes veniant.*
I am afraid that the enemy is coming.

*Timebam **ne** hostes venirent.*
I was afraid that the enemy was coming.

*Timeo **ne** hostes venerint.*
I am afraid that the enemy has come.

*Timebam **ne** hostes venissent.*
I was afraid that the enemy had come.

*Timeo **ut** amici veniant.*
I am afraid that the friends are not coming.

• *Clauses after non dubito quin*

Clauses after *non dubito quin, nemo dubitat quin* are extended direct objects of the main clause. They are constructed with the subjunctive according to the rules of the sequence of tenses. Posteriority is expressed by the periphrastic conjugation.

*Non dubito **quin** tu plus provideas.*
I do not doubt that you see farther ahead.

*Nemo dubitat **quin** sis venturus.*
Nobody doubts that you will come.

- ## *Clauses after verbs of preventing and refusing*

After verbs of preventing and refusing (*impedio, recuso, prohibeo, obsto*) we use an extended object clause introduced by *quin* (only after a negative statement), *ne* (only after an affirmative statement), or *quominus* (after either a negative or affirmative statement). These clauses are constructed with the subjunctive according to the rules of the sequence of tenses.

*Plura **ne** scribam dolor impedit.*
The pain hinders me from writing more.

*Quid obstat **quominus** sis beatus?*
What prevents you from being happy?

*Nihil impedit **quin** id facere possimus.*
There is no hindrance to our doing this.

*Te dolor tenuit **quominus** venires.*
The pain kept you from coming.

2. Adjectival or attributive clauses

We use adjectival clauses in order to give more information about a noun in the main clause. Thus, an adjectival clause is an extended adjective or attribute modifying a noun of the main clause. Most adjectival clauses are explicit relative clauses. An attributive participle is an implicit adjectival clause.

• *Relative clauses*

Relative clauses are introduced by the relative pronoun *qui, quae, quod*. The relative pronoun agrees in number and in gender with the noun in the main clause to which it refers.

*Malum est consilium **quod** mutari non potest.*
A plan which cannot be changed is a bad one.

Relative clauses may also be introduced by the indefinite relative pronouns *quicumque, quaecumque, quodcumque* and *quisquis, quidquid (quicquid)*.

***Quidquid** id est, timeo Danaos et dona ferentes.*
Whatever it is, I fear the Danai, even if they bring presents.

Relative clauses may be introduced by the relative adverbs *ut, quantum, quanti, quanto, ubi, quo, unde, qua, quamdiu, quotiens* as well.

*Illuc **unde** abii redeo.*
I return to the place I came from.

Relative clauses are usually constructed with the indicative. However, the subjunctive may be used in them in the same way as in main clauses, to express possibility or wish.

*Habeo **quae** velim.*
I have everything I would possibly like to.

- ## *Attributive participle*

The attributive participle functions practically as an adjectival implicit clause.

*Epistulam a patre **missam** legi. (=Epistulam quam pater miserat legi.)*
I read the letter sent by the father. (=I read the letter which the father had sent).

3. Adverbial or circumstantial clauses

Adverbial or circumstantial clauses are logically expanded adverbs modifying the main verb. We use them when we need to add an expanded circumstance to the verb of the main clause. The circumstances may be of the following types:
a) time;
b) cause;
c) purpose;
d) result;
e) concession;
f) condition;
g) comparison;
h) contrast;
i) restriction.

For each of these circumstances, a specific sort of clause is used.

a) How to express a temporal circumstance.

We express temporal circumstances most often by explicit clauses constructed with the indicative. If we use the subjunctive, it is usually to indicate that the action is potential or repeated. The participle construction and the ablative absolute are implicit clauses expressing temporal circumstances.

α)   *The subordinate and the main action take place at the same time*

- Cum *with the indicative.*

Cum with the indicative points to a general chronological coincidence between two actions, usually repeated.

Iudex damnatur, **cum** *nocens absolvitur.*
The judge is condemned when someone guilty is acquitted.

- *The historical* cum *with the imperfect subjunctive.*

Cum with the imperfect subjunctive narrates an action in the past, during which the action of the main clause took place.

Cum *essem Brundisii, litteras tuas accepi.*
While I was in Brundisium, I received your letter.

However, it rarely presents only a temporal circumstance. More often, the temporal nuance is combined with a causal one.

Haec **cum** *ita essent, Caesar exploratores misit.*
Since the situation was such, Caesar sent spies.

- Dum *with the indicative.*

Dum with the indicative indicates an action contemporaneous with the main one, but whose beginning and end do not necessarily coincide with the beginning and end of the main one.

49

Dum *Romae consulitur, Saguntum expugnatur.*
While people confer in Rome, Saguntum is taken by assault. (a
sentence that has become proverbial, from Livy's account of the
Second Punic War)

- Dum, donec, quoad *with the indicative.*

Dum, donec and *quoad* with the indicative may indicate an action
which begins and ends, or at least ends, at the same time as the action
in the main clause.

Donec *felix eris, multos numerabis amicos.*
As long as you are blessed by fortune, you will have many friends.

- *Clauses with* quotiens *and* quotienscumque.

We use clauses with *quotiens* and *quotienscumque* to indicate a
circumstance which occurs repeatedly and along with which, whenever
it happens, the main action takes place as well. These are usually
constructed with the indicative.

Quotienscumque *loquor, in iudicium ingenii venio.*
Every time I speak, my intelligence is being judged.

- *Participle construction with the present participle.*

The present participle may be used as an implicit temporal clause and
indicate an action contemporaneous with the action of the main clause.

Occisus est a cena **rediens**. *(=Occisus est, cum a cena rediret.)*
He was killed while he was coming back from dinner.

- *Ablative absolute with the present participle.*

The ablative absolute with the present participle usually indicates an
action contemporaneous with the action in the main clause.

Crescente pecunia crescit avaritia. (=Cum pecunia crescit, crescit avaritia).
When money grows, greed grows as well.

The ablative absolute with a noun (indicating age or office) also indicates an action or state contemporaneous with the action in the main clause.

Cicerone consule facta est coniuratio. (=Cum Cicero consul esset, facta est coniuratio).
When Cicero was a consul, a plot was hatched.

β) *The subordinate action limits the main one*

- Dum, donec, quoad *with the indicative.*

Clauses with *dum, donec, quoad* may indicate an action with whose end the action in the main clause begins. These clauses are usually constructed with the indicative.

Dum rediit, fuit silentium.
There was silence until he returned.

- Dum, donec, quoad *with the subjunctive.*

The clauses with *dum, donec, quoad* may indicate an action which not only limits the main verb in time, but represents also its purpose. In this case they are constructed with the subjunctive.

Dum mihi a te litterae veniant, in Italia morabor.
I will remain in Italy until I receive a letter from you.

γ) *The subordinate action precedes the main one*

- *The historical* cum *with the pluperfect subjunctive.*

We use *cum* with the pluperfect subjunctive to indicate an action which occurred before the action in the main clause.

Cum *haec dixisset, silentium est consecutum.*
After he said that, silence followed.

• *Clauses with* postquam.

We may use clauses with *postquam*, constructed with the perfect or, more rarely, the pluperfect indicative, to indicate an action which occurred before the action in the main clause.

Postquam *te aspexit, extimuit.*
After he saw you, he feared greatly.

• *Participle construction with the perfect participle.*

The perfect participle may be used as an implicit temporal clause indicating an action preceding the main action.

Terra **mutata** *mutavit mores. (=Postquam terra mutata est, mutavit mores.)*
The earth, having been changed itself, changed customs.

• *Ablative absolute with the perfect participle.*

The ablative absolute with a perfect participle may function practically as a temporal clause indicating an action which precedes the action in the main clause.

Urbe expugnata *imperator rediit. (=Postquam urbs expugnata est, imperator rediit).*
Having taken the city by assault, the commander returned.

δ) *The subordinate action immediately precedes the main one*

- *Clauses with* cum primum, simul ac, ubi (primum), ut (primum)

We use the clauses with *cum primum, simul ac, ubi (primum), ut (primum)* to indicate an action which immediately precedes the action of the main clause. They are usually constructed with the indicative.

Cum primum *potuit, Caesar ad exercitum contendit.*
As soon as he could, Caesar rushed to the army.

Simul ac *constituero, ad te scribam.*
As soon as I decide, I will write you.

Ubi *dux dixit, milites conclamaverunt.*
As soon as the commander finished his speech, the soldiers shouted together.

Ut *Romam venit, praetor factus est.*
As soon as he came to Rome, he became a praetor.

ε) *The subordinate action happens after the main one*

- *Clauses with* priusquam *and* antequam

Clauses with *priusquam* and *antequam* express an action which will or would happen after the main action. They are usually constructed with the indicative, but sometimes with the subjunctive, especially if the action is potential. If these clauses refer to the present, they are constructed with the present indicative, the perfect indicative, or the present subjunctive. If they refer to the past, they are constructed with the perfect indicative or the imperfect subjunctive. If they refer to the future, they are constructed with the present indicative, the present subjunctive, or the future perfect.

*Fulgorem cernimus **antequam** tonitrum accipimus.*
We see the lightning before we hear the thunder.

*Hostes fugere non destiterunt **priusquam** ad flumen advenerunt.*
The enemy did not stop fleeing until they reached the river.

*Collem celeriter communivit **priusquam** ab adversariis sentiretur.*
He quickly fortified the hill before the enemies could hear him.

***Antequam** de re publica dicam, de me enarrabo.*
Before speaking about the state, I will speak about myself.

ç) *The subordinate action changes radically what the main action has done*

- *Clauses with the inverse* cum

Clauses with the inverse *cum* are used to change radically what has nearly happened in the main clause. They are usually constructed with the perfect indicative, while the main clause has the indicative in a past tense, and often contains one of these adverbs: *iam, vix, aegre, prope, nondum.*

*Romani prope Pyrrhum vicerunt, **cum** elephanti procucurrerunt.*
The Romans had almost defeated Pyrrhus when all of a sudden the elephants ran forth.

b) How to express a causal circumstance.

We may express a causal circumstance with either an explicit or an implicit clause. Some of the conjunctions introducing explicit clauses require the subjunctive; other require either the indicative or the subjunctive: the indicative if the cause is conceived as objective, the subjunctive if the cause is a subjective one. The subjunctive follows the rules of the sequence of tenses.

- *Clauses with* quod *and* quia

Clauses with *quod* and *quia* are constructed with the indicative when the clause is conceived as an objective one, and with the subjunctive when it is conceived as subjective.
We use *quod* to express the cause after the verbs of emotion (*gaudeo, doleo, laudo, gratias ago, aegre fero, irascor, accuso*). This cause may also be expressed by the accusative and infinitive construction (see *1. Substantive or complementary clauses, Accusative with infinitive*).

*Nemo patriam **quia** magna est amat, sed quia sua.*
One does not love one's fatherland because of its size, but because it is one's own.

*Agunt gratias **quod** sibi pepercissent.*
They are thankful that they have been spared. (It is their perception that they have been spared.)

- *Clauses with* quoniam *and* quando

Causal clauses with *quoniam* and *quando* usually point to an obvious and known reason and are constructed with the indicative.

***Quoniam** iam est nox, in tecta vestra discedite!*
Since it is already dark, go back to your homes!

*Voluptas semovenda est, **quando** ad maiora quaedam nati sumus.*
Pleasure should be set aside, for we were born for more important purposes.

- *Clauses with the causal* cum

Causal clauses with *cum* usually give the motivation for the action in the main clause and are always constructed with the subjunctive.

Cum *id facere non possem, quievi.*
Since I could not do this, I abstained from action.

- *Relative causal clauses*

We may use a relative circumstantial clause, always constructed with the subjunctive, in order to express a causal circumstance. The relative pronoun is often preceded by *quippe, utpote* or *ut*.

Eos libros non contemno, **quippe** *quos numquam legerim.*
I do not despise these books since I have never read them.

- *Participle construction*

We may use a participle construction as an implicit causal clause. However, its more frequent use is the temporal one.

His nuntiis **commotus** *Caesar duas legiones conscripsit.*
Being upset by this news, Caesar enlisted two legions.

c) How to express purpose.

We may express purpose with explicit clauses constructed with the subjunctive following the rules of the sequence of tenses, i.e., with the present subjunctive or the imperfect subjunctive, or we may do it with implicit clauses.

- *Clauses with the final* ut

The most frequent way of expressing purpose is by using a clause with the final *ut*. When the clause is negative, we use the final *ne*.

*Non **ut** edam vivo, sed **ut** vivam edo.*
I do not live in order to eat, but eat in order to live.

*Viatores non eunt **ut** eant.*
Travellers do not walk merely for the sake of walking.

*Nolo esse laudator **ne** videar adulator.*
I do not want to be a praiser, for fear I may seem a flatterer.

*Legati venerunt **ut** pacem peterent.*
Ambassadors came to ask for peace.

- *Purpose clauses with* quo

When there is an adjective in the comparative degree in a statement of purpose, we do not use *ut*, but *quo*.

*Legem brevem esse oportet **quo** facilius ab imperitis teneatur.*
The law should be short in order to be remembered more easily by non-experts.

- *Relative purpose clauses*

We may use a relative circumstantial clause, always constructed with the subjunctive, in order to express purpose.

*Legati missi sunt **qui** pacem **peterent**.*
Ambassadors were sent to ask for peace.

- *Gerund or gerundive construction (ad with the accusative of the gerund or with the gerundive)*

Ad with the accusative of the gerund or with the gerundive may be used to denote purpose. When the verb to be put in the gerund or gerundive has a direct object, normally the gerundive is used; if not, the gerund is used.

Ad dissimulandum *paratus est.*
He is ready to pretend.

Ad foedus faciendum *duces prodeunt.*
The commanders come forth in order to make an agreement.

- *Future active participle*

We may use the future active participle as an implicit purpose clause.

Venit pacem ***petiturus****.*
He comes to ask for peace.

- *Accusative supine*

The accusative supine expresses purpose, but we may use it in this function only after verbs of motion.

Cubitum *eo.*
I am going to bed.

Spectatum *veniunt, veniunt spectentur ut ipsae.*
They come to watch; they come to be watched. (Ovid about the Roman women in the theater).

d) How to express a result.

Result may be expressed only with explicit clauses. They are constructed with the subjunctive, and they do not follow the rule of the sequence of tenses. To indicate result in the present or a possible or desired result in the future, we use the present subjunctive. To indicate result in the past, we use the imperfect subjunctive if the action is presented as lasting or potential, and the perfect subjunctive if the action is presented as accomplished.

In the main clause we normally use one of the following words: *sic, ita, tam, tantus, talis, is, adeo*.

•   *Clauses with the consecutive* ut

The most frequent way of expressing a result is to use a clause with the consecutive *ut*. If the result is negative, we use *ut non* or, rarely, *quin*.

*Nemo adeo ferus est **ut non** mitescere **possit***.
Nobody is so cruel that he cannot become milder.

*Ita vixi **ut** me **non** frustra natum **existimem***.
I lived in such a way that I can believe myself not to have been born in vain.

*Ille sic Graece loquebatur **ut** Athenis natus **videretur***.
He spoke Greek in such a manner that he seemed to have been born in Athens.

*Cleopatra erat tantae pulchritudinis **ut** multi illius noctem morte **emerint***.
Cleopatra was of such beauty that many men paid with death to spend a night with her.

*Numquam tam male est Siculis **quin** aliquid facete et commode **dicant***.
For the Sicilians, never are things so bad that they cannot say something humorous or pleasant.

- *Relative result clauses (also called relative clauses of characteristic)*

After certain expressions, relative result clauses are normally used. The most important of these expressions are the following:

sunt qui
non sunt qui
reperiuntur qui
inveniuntur qui
nemo est qui
nihil est quod
quis est qui
solus est qui

Relative result clauses are also used after the adjectives *dignus, indignus, aptus* and *idoneus.*

Sunt **quibus** *in satura videar nimis acer.*
There are some people to whom I seem too sharp in my satires.

Dignus est **qui** *laudetur.*
He is worthy of praise.

Haec sola res est **quae** *nos adiuvare possit.*
This is the only thing which can help us.

e) How to express a concession.

We may express a concession with either explicit or implicit clauses. Some of the conjunctions used for concessions require the subjunctive; others may be used either with the indicative or with the subjunctive, depending on whether the concession is real, or it is possible or conceived as subjective. The subjunctive follows the rules of the sequence of tenses.

In the main clause we may use the adverbs *tamen, attamen, nihilominus, certe* in the sense of "nevertheless."

- *Clauses with* quamquam, quamvis, licet, etsi, etiamsi, tametsi

Quamquam usually requires the indicative and points to a real concession. *Quamvis* and *licet* express a concession conceived as subjective and require the subjunctive. *Etsi, etiamsi* and *tametsi* may require either the indicative or, more frequently, the subjunctive, depending on whether the concession is a fact, or it is possible or conceived as subjective.

Quamquam *omnis virtus nos ad se allicit, tamen iustitia hoc maxime efficit.*
Although every virtue attracts us, nevertheless justice does so most of all.

Licet *omnes fremant, dicam quod sentio.*
Though all may murmur, I will say what I feel.

Vitia mentis, **quamvis** *exigua sint, in maius excedunt.*
Imperfections of the mind, even if they may be small, tend to increase.

Inops **etiamsi** *referre gratiam non potest, habere certe potest.*
Even if the poor person is not able to return a favor, he can at least be grateful.

Utilitas efflorescit ex amicitia, **etiamsi** *tu eam minus secutus sis.*
Some advantage springs up from friendship, even if you have not looked for it.

- *Clauses with the concessive* ut

The concessive *ut* always requires the subjunctive. The negation is *ne*.

Ut desint vires, tamen est laudanda voluntas.
Although strength may fail, the intention is to be praised.

Ne sit sane summum malum dolor, malum certe est.
Even if pain is not be the supreme evil, it is certainly an evil.

- *Clauses with the concessive* cum

The concessive *cum* always requires the subjunctive.

Socrates, **cum** *facile posset educi e custodia, noluit.*
Although Socrates might easily have been led out of the prison, he did not want to be.

- *Relative concessive clauses*

We may also express concession with a relative circumstantial clause, which is always constructed with the subjunctive.

Hic, **qui** *in collegio sacerdotum esset, est condemnatus.*
Even though he was a member of a college of priests, he was condemned.

- *Participle construction*

We may use a participle construction as an implicit concessive clause.

Risus interdum ita repente erumpit ut eum **cupientes** *tenere nequeamus.*
Sometimes laughter bursts forth so suddenly that we cannot hold it back even though we want to.

f) *How to express a condition.*

● *Conditions with* si

We usually express a condition with an explicit clause introduced by *si*. If the condition is negative, the clause is introduced by *nisi* if the negation refers to the whole clause and thus limits the main clause, and by *si non* if the negation refers only to one word of the subordinate clause.

*Hoc **nisi** feceris, te non amabo.*
I won't love you, unless you do it.

*Hoc **si non** optimum, at certe bonum est.*
Even if this is not the best, it is certainly good.

The main clause, which indicates what happens if the condition is fulfilled, usually has the same tense and mood as the *si*-clause. Various moods and tenses are used, according to how realizable the condition is, and whether past, present, or future time is referred to.

1) When we are not concerned about whether the condition is realizable or not, we use the indicative both in the main and in the *si*-clause.

***Si** nummos **habeo, emo** currum. (Nescitur utrum nummos habeam necne....)*
If I have some money, I buy a car.

2) When the condition is realizable, we use the present subjunctive or the perfect subjunctive both in the main and in the *si*-clause.

***Si** nummos **habeam, emam** currum. (Et forsitan nummos habebo....)*
***Si** nummos **habuerim, emerim** currum. (Et forsitan nummos habebo....)*
If I get some money, I will buy a car.

The difference between the use of the present subjunctive and the perfect subjunctive is one of aspect. Aspect, which manifests itself in Latin only in the distinction between the present potential subjunctive and the perfect potential subjunctive, involves the distinction between action presented as lasting and unfulfilled (incomplete aspect) and action presented as momentary and accomplished (complete aspect).

Si nummos habeam, emam currum. (Si cras, perendie, post hebdomadem, post mensem, post annum....)
Si nummos habuerim, emerim currum. (Si cras, cum ad tabernam ivero....).

3) When the condition is not realizable in the present, we use the imperfect subjunctive both in the main and in the *si*-clause.

Si nummos haberem, emerem *currum. (Si nummos haberem nunc.... Tamen non habeo....)*
If I had some money, I would buy a car.

4) When the condition is not realized in the past, we use the pluperfect subjunctive both in the main and in the *si*-clause.

Si *nummos* **habuissem, emissem** *currum. (Si nummos habuissem heri.... Tamen non habui....)*
If I had got some money, I would have bought a car.

- *Participle construction*

We may use a participle as an implicit condition.

Nec rogemus res turpes nec faciamus **rogati**.
We should not ask indecent things, neither should we do them if we are asked.

• *Conditional-proviso clauses with* dum, dummodo, modo

If we want to express a condition accompanied by the notion of a wish or proviso "as long as", "provided that", we construct a clause introduced by *dum, dummodo*, or *modo*. The negation is *ne*. These clauses are constructed with the subjunctive which follows the rules of the sequence of tenses.

*Oderint, **dum** metuant.*
Let them hate me, provided they fear me.

*Tu mihi scribas velim, **dummodo ne** his verbis scribas.*
I would like you to write me, provided you do not write with these words.

g) How to make a comparison.

We can make a comparison using explicit clauses that are usually constructed with the indicative. If we need to indicate a potential action or add a nuance of subjectivity, the subjunctive should be used.

• *Comparison of manner*

A comparison of manner is made using a clause introduced by *ut, sicut, velut, quemadmodum, tamquam.*

Ut salutaveris, ita salutaberis.
As you greet, so will you be greeted.

• *Comparison of quantity or intensity*

A comparison of quantity, size, intensity, or price is made using a clause introduced by *quam, quantus, quantum, quanto, quanti, quot.*

Quot *homines, tot sententiae.*
There are as many opinions as there are people.

● *Comparison of identity and difference*

A comparison of identity or difference is made using a clause introduced by *atque* (*ac*) usually following adjectives or adverbs expressing likeness or unlikeness.

Hic loquebatur aliter **atque** *omnes.*
He was speaking in a different way from the other people.

● *Comparison of degree*

A comparison of degree is made using a clause introduced by *quam*.

Plus tibi virtus tua dedit **quam** *fortuna abstulit.*
Your virtue has given you more than destiny has taken from you.

● *Conditional comparison*

To express a conditional comparison, we use clauses constructed with *ut si, velut si, ac si, quam si, tamquam si, tamquam, quasi* and *velut*. These clauses are constructed with the subjunctive. The use of the tenses of the subjunctive is the same as for *si*-clauses (i.e., the present or the perfect subjunctive for a realizable condition, the imperfect subjunctive for a non-realizable condition, and the pluperfect subjunctive for an unrealized condition).

Sic vivendum est **tamquam** *in conspectu viveremus.*
We need to live as we lived within the sight of every one.

h) How to express a contrast.

We express a contrast to the action of the main clause with a clause introduced by the adversative *cum* and the subjunctive, following the rules of the sequence of tenses.

Cum *animalia cetera terram spectarent, os homini sublime dedit.*
Whereas all the animals looked at the ground, he (the creator) gave to man an upraised face.

i) How to express a restriction.

In order to restrict the action of the main clause, we use a clause introduced by *ut, quoad, quatenus, quantum, quam, quod.* These clauses are usually constructed with the indicative, except for the *quod*-clauses, which can be constructed with the subjunctive as well.

Ille patre usus est, **ut** *tum erant tempora, diti.*
He had the advantage of a rich father, at least according to the standards of the time.

Id faciam, **quoad** *fieri potest.*
I will do this as far as it can be done.

Quod *sciam, orator est optimus.*
As far as I know, he is an excellent speaker.

4. Conjunctions and clauses apt to express different relation to the main clause

As can be gathered from the preceding discussion, some very common conjunctions have multiple functions; thus a single conjunction can serve to introduce various sorts of subordinate clauses, and in some cases to create coordinate links between clauses as well. For convenience, these multiple uses of certain conjunctions and constructions are summarized below.

a) Ut

- in exclamatory questions
- explicative
- objective
- = *ne non* after verbs of fearing
- temporal
- final
- consecutive
- concessive
- comparative
- restrictive.

b) Ne

- a part of the negative conjunction *ne ... quidem*
- objective
- after verbs of fearing
- after verbs of preventing and refusing
- final
- concessive.

c) Cum

- temporal (historical, inverse)
- causal
- concessive
- adversative.

d) Dum

- temporal
- introducing conditional-proviso clauses.

e) Atque (ac)

- copulative conjunction
- comparative.

f) Quin

- after *non dubito, dubium non est*, etc.
- after verbs of preventing and refusing
- consecutive.

g) Quod

- relative pronoun neuter nominative and accusative
- explicative
- causal
- restrictive.

h) Quam

- comparative
- restrictive.

i) Quo

- relative pronoun masculine and neuter ablative singular
- final.

j) Quoad

- temporal
- restrictive.

k) Relative clauses

- attributive
- causal
- final
- consecutive
- concessive.

l) Participle construction

- attributive
- temporal
- causal
- final
- concessive
- conditional.

Chapter IV
The Indirect Discourse

To report someone else's words, we may use either the direct discourse or the indirect discourse. In the first case, we report the words just as they were spoken by the original speaker; in the second, we report them indirectly, adapted to our own point of view. Here we will observe the transformation of the direct discourse into the indirect discourse.

1. Main clauses (simple and coordinate)

- The declarative sentences (statements of fact, negative statements of fact, statements of possibility and counterfactual statements) become accusative with infinitive. Statements of fact and negative statements of fact follow the rule of using the tenses in accusative with infinitive clauses (see *III. Subordination, 1. Substantive or complementary clauses, Accusative with infinitive*). The possibility-indicating subjunctive (the present and the perfect subjunctive) becomes a future infinitive. The unreality-indicating subjunctive (the imperfect and the pluperfect subjunctive) becomes a perfect infinitive of the periphrastic conjugation.

"Historia est", ait Cicero, "magistra vitae." →
*Cicero dicebat **historiam esse magistram** vitae.*
Cicero said that history is a teacher of life.

"Non facile domum relinquerim", inquit.→
*Dixit non facile **se** domum **esse relicturum**.*
He said that he would not easily abandon his home.

"Sine auxilio non vicissem", inquit.→
*Dixit sine auxilio **se non fuisse victurum***
He said that he would not have won without help.

- In the indirect discourse, question, doubt and deliberation clauses become clauses with the subjunctive following the rules of sequence of tenses.

"Quid vis?", me rogat (rogavit).→
*Rogat me quid **velim**.*
He is asking me what I want.
*Rogavit me quid **vellem**.*
He asked me what I wanted.

"Quo nos miselli ibimus?", dubitant (dubitabant).→
*Dubitant quo ipsi miselli **eant**.*
They don't know where they should go in their misery.
*Dubitabant quo ipsi miselli **irent**.*
They didn't know where they should go in their misery.

- In the indirect discourse, rhetorical questions become accusative with infinitive clauses.

"Cui hic dolus non patet?", interrogo. (= Hic dolus omnibus patet.)→
*Interrogo cui **hunc dolum non patere**.*
I ask to whom this fraud is not obvious.

- In the indirect discourse, the imperative sentences (expressing command, prohibition, exhortation, wish, and concession) become clauses with the subjunctive following the rules of sequence of tenses.

"Relinquite arma!" or *"Relinquatis arma!" exclamat (exclamavit).→*
Exclamat: Arma **relinquant**.
He shouts them an order to leave the weapons.
Exclamavit: Arma **relinquerent**.
He shouted them an order to leave the weapons.

• In the indirect discourse, the exclamatory sentences become accusative with infinitive clauses.

"Tam diserte loqueris!" mirabar.→
Mirabar: **Illum** *tam diserte* **loqui**.
I wondered that he was speaking so clearly.

2. Subordinate clauses

Subordinate clauses, either with the indicative or with the subjunctive, become clauses with the subjunctive following the rules of sequence of tenses.

"Florem aetatis", inquit Hanno, "Hasdrubal, quem ipse patri Hannibalis fruendum **praebuit**, *iusto iure eum a filio repeti censet."→*
Florem aetatis Hasdrubalem, quem ipse patri Hannibalis fruendum **praebuisset**, *iusto iure eum a filio repeti censere.*
Hanno said that Hasdrubal thought that he could ask back from the son (Hannibal, Hamilcar's son) with perfect justice the same youthful age he himself had given for use to the father of Hannibal (Hamilcar, Hannibal's father).
[Hanno was the leader of the opposition party in Carthage. Hasdrubal was Hamilcar's son-in-law, who had advanced his military career under the command of Hamilcar].

3. Pronouns

- *Ego* and *nos* in nominative become *ipse, ipsa, ipsi, ipsae*; in the other cases, they become *sui, sibi, se*.
- *Meus* and *noster* in nominative become *ipsius, ipsorum, ipsarum*; in the other cases, they become *suus*.
- *Tu* and *vos* become *ille* or *is*.
- *Tuus* and *vester* become *illius, illorum* or *eius, eorum*.
- *Hic* and *iste* are avoided and are usually replaced by *is* and *ille*.

*"**Ego istum** iuvenem,"* *dixit Hanno,* *"domi tenendum sub legibus, sub magistratibus, docendum vivere aequo iure cum ceteris censeo."*→
***Se illum** iuvenem domi tenendum sub legibus, sub magistratibus, docendum vivere aequo iure cum ceteris censere.*
Hanno said that he thought that this young man (Hannibal) should be kept at home under the control of law and administrators and should be taught to live in the same way as the others.

*"Saguntum **vestri** circumsedent exercitus unde arcentur foedere; mox Carthaginem circumsedebunt Romanae legiones",* *dicebat Hanno.* →
*Saguntum **illorum** exercitus circumsedere, unde arcerentur foedere; mox Carthaginem circumsessuras Romanas legiones.*
Hanno said that in that moment their army was besieging Saguntum, where it was not allowed according to the agreement; soon the Roman legions would besiege Carthage. (Hanno against Hannibal's siege of Saguntum.)

4. Adverbs

- *Hodie* becomes *eo* or *illo die*.
- *Cras* becomes *postero die* or *postridie*.
- *Heri* becomes *pridie*.
- *Nunc* becomes *tunc*.
- *Adhuc* becomes *ad id tempus*.
- *Hic* becomes *illic*.

"*Carthagini* **nunc** *Hannibal vineas turresque admovet;*" *monet Hanno,* "*Carthaginis moenia quatit ariete.*" →
Carthagini **tunc** *Hannibalem vineas turresque admovere. Carthaginis moenia quatere ariete.*
Hanno warns that now Hannibal moves sheds and towers to Carthage, that now he shakes with a battering-ram the city walls of Carthage. (about the siege of Saguntum by Hannibal)

5. Conditional clauses

Here are the changes of the conditional clauses in the indirect discourse.

- *Si nummos habeo, emo currum.* →
Dico **me** *currum* **emere**, *si nummos* **habeam**.
Dixi **me** *currum* **emere**, *si nummos* **haberem**.

- *Si nummos habeam, emam currum.* →
Dico **me** *currum* **esse empturum**, *si nummos* **habeam**.
Dixi **me** *currum* **esse empturum**, *si nummos* **haberem**.

- *Si nummos habuerim, emerim currum.* →
Dico **me** *currum* **esse empturum**, *si nummos* **habuerim**.
Dixi **me** *currum* **esse empturum**, *si nummos* **habuissem**.

- *Si nummos haberem, emerem currum.* →
Dico (dixi) **me** *currum* **fuisse empturum**, *si nummos* **haberem**.

- *Si nummos habuissem, emissem currum.* →
Dico (dixi) **me** *currum* **fuisse empturum**, *si nummos* **habuissem**.

Chapter V
Relations within a clause

1. Subject and agent (quis? quid?)

- The person or the thing that performs the action is in the nominative. All modifiers and appositives that refer to that person or thing are in the nominative as well.

Deus mundum gubernat.
God governs the world.

Amicus certus in re incerta cernitur.
A friend in need is a friend indeed.

Cato senex litteras Graecas didicit.
Cato learned the Greek language when an old man.

- When the predicate is made up of a copulative verb and a predicate noun or adjective, the predicate noun or adjective is in the nominative as well.

Scientia est potentia.
Knowledge is power.

Fortuna caeca est.
Fortune is blind.

Res difficilis videtur.
The thing seems to be difficult.

*Cicero **consul** creatus est.*
Cicero was elected consul.

- The agent (which is the logical subject) with the passive voice is denoted by the preposition *ab* and the ablative if it is animate, and with the simple ablative if it is inanimate.

*Non semper viator **a latrone**, nonnumquam latro **a viatore** occiditur.*
The traveller is not always killed by a brigand; sometimes the brigand is killed by the traveller.

*Biduo **tempestate** est retentus.*
He was detained for two days by a storm.

- The agent of the verb in the passive periphrastic coniugation is in the dative.

*Epistula **mihi** scribenda est.*
I have to write a letter.

2. Direct object (quem? quid?)

The direct object, i.e., the person or the thing to whom or to which the action of the transitive verbs passes directly, is expressed by the accusative.

***Fortes** fortuna adiuvat.*
Fortune helps the courageous.

*Graecia capta **ferum victorem** cepit.*
Captured Greece captivated her cruel conquerer (Rome).

3. Indirect object (cui?)

- The indirect object, i.e., the person or the thing to which the action refers indirectly, is expressed by the dative.

*Vir bonus **multis** prodest, nocet **nemini**.*
The honest man is of use to many people and is harmful to no one.

*Facile omnes, cum valemus, recta consilia **aegrotis** damus.*
All of us, when in good health, easily give good advice to ill people.

- A person or a thing for whose benefit or disadvantage the action takes place or a person who is somehow involved in the action, even emotionally, is also indicated by the dative.

*Non **scholae**, sed **vitae** discimus.*
We learn not for school, but for life.

*Ubi **mihi** est filius?*
Where is my son?

- A person in whose eyes or in respect to whom the statement of the sentence is true is also indicated by the dative.

*Quintia formosa est **multis**.*
Quintia is beautiful in the eyes of many people.

*Hoc est oppidum primum Thessaliae **venientibus** ab Epiro.*
This is the first town in Thessaly for those who come from Epirus.

4. Possession (cuius?)

To emphasize possession, we put the person or thing possessed in the nominative, the possessor in the dative and use the verb *esse*. If the possessor is to be emphasized, it is expressed by the genitive.

Natura est **omnibus** *una.*
Everybody has one and the same nature.

Domus **patris** *est ampla.*
The house of the father is big.

Opera **Ciceronis** *lego.*
I read Cicero's works.

The possession for first and second person is indicated by a possessive adjective.

liber **meus**
my book

5. Specification (cuius? cuius rei?)

When the sense of a noun is to be rendered more specific by another noun, the noun providing the specification is put into the genitive.

Veritatis *simplex oratio est.*
The language of truth is simple.

Consuetudinis *magna vis est.*
Great is the force of habit.

6. Subjective and objective specification (cuius?)

Subjective or objective specification to a substantive derived from a verb (such a substantive contains the idea of an action) is expressed by the genitive.

amor Dei = Deus amat
amor Dei = amor erga Deum, Deus amatur

filii parvi *desiderium* **mei**
my little son's longing for me

The subjective genitive is used only in the third person. In the first and second person the possessive adjective is used.

filii parvi desiderium **meum**
my longing for my little son

7. Place

a) Location (ubi?)

- We usually indicate location with the preposition *in* and the ablative.

Histrio **in scaena** *est.*
The actor is on the stage.

- The movement within a certain place is also conceived as location and we indicate it with *in* and the ablative.

***In horto** ambulabam.*
I was walking in the garden.

- The names of towns, villages, and small islands, are expressed by the locative if the name belongs to the first or second declension; however, if the name belongs to the third declension, or it belongs to the first or second, but is used only in the plural, it is expressed by the simple ablative. Furthermore, if such a name is accompanied by an appositive, we put it in the ablative preceded by the preposition *in*.

***Romae, Mediolani, Carthagine, Athenis** commoror.*
I stop off in Rome, Milan, Carthage, Athens.

***In urbe Roma** sum natus.*
I was born in the city of Rome.

- The word *domus*, when used alone or with a possessive adjective to indicate location, is put into the locative. However, if it is accompanied by an ordinary adjective, it is put into the ablative preceded by the preposition *in*. The word *rus*, when used to indicate location, should be in the locative as well.

***Domi** maneo.*
I remain at home.

***Ruri** beate vivitur.*
People live happily in the countryside.

domi suae
at his (her) home

in domo ampla
in a big home

- To indicate location, the word *locus* is put into the simple ablative when modified by an adjective.

idoneo loco
in a convenient place

- All substantives used to indicate location and modified by the adjectives *totus* and *omnis* are put into the simple ablative.

toto mundo
in the whole world

omnibus oppidis
in every town

- The phrase *terra marique* (= by land and by sea) is used in the simple ablative.

b) Direction (quo?)

- We usually indicate direction with the accusative preceded by the preposition *in* (which implies entering a certain place) or by the preposition *ad* (which implies only an approaching).

*Confugimus **in fanum**.*
We found refuge in the sanctuary.

***Ad montes** sumus profecti.*
We left for the mountains.

- Direction towards towns, villages, and small islands, as well as with the words *rus* and *domus*, is expressed by the simple accusative. *Domum* is so used when it is modified by a possessive adjective, but not when modified by an ordinary adjective.

*Eo **Romam, Mediolanum, Athenas, Neapolim, domum, rus***.
I go to Rome, Milan, Athens, Naples, home, the countryside.

*Eo **domum meam***.
I am going home.

*Eo **in domum amplam***.
I am going to a big house.

c) *Movement away (unde?)*

We usually indicate movement away with the ablative preceded by the preposition *a* (*ab* or *abs*), if it implies a general separation, with the ablative preceded by the preposition *e* (*ex*) if an exit is implied, and with the ablative preceded by the preposition *de* if a downward movement is implied.

***Ab uxore** tabellarius venit*.
There came a letter-carrier from my wife.

*Egredere **ex urbe**!*
Get out of the city!

*Araneas deiciam **de pariete***.
I will remove the cobwebs from the wall.

- Departure from towns, villages, and small islands, as well as with the word *rus* and the word *domus*, the latter also accompanied by pronouns but not by adjectives, is expressed by the simple ablative.

***Roma, Mediolano, Athenis, Neapoli, domo, rure** proficiscor*.
I depart from Rome, Milan, Athens, Naples, from home, from the countryside.

***Domo mea** proficiscor.*
I depart from my home.

***Ex domo ampla** proficiscor.*
I depart from a big house.

d) Passing through (qua?)

A place through which a movement passes is expressed by the accusative preceded by the preposition *per*; however, if the passage is restricted, e.g., a door, a road, or a bridge, it is expressed by the simple ablative.

***Per silvas** profectus est.*
He set out through the woods.

*Ibam forte **via Sacra**.*
I happened to be walking along the Sacra Via.

Here we summarize the use of some adverbs indicating location, direction, movement away, and passing through, with reference to different locations.

- Near the person who is speaking:
  hic - huc - hinc - hac;
- Near the person who is being addressed:
  istic - istuc - istinc - istac;
- Near the person about whom we are speaking:
  illic - illuc - illinc - illac;
- In a generally indicated place:
  ibi - eo - unde - ea;
- In the same place indicated previously:
  ibidem - eodem - indidem - eadem;

- In a place we are asking about:
  ubi? - quo? - unde? - qua?
- In a place indicated in the main clause and specified in a relative clause:
  ubi - quo - unde - qua;
- In another place:
  alibi - alio - aliunde - alia;
- In whatever place:
  ubicumque - quocumque - undecumque - quacumque;
- In an uncertain place:
  alicubi - aliquo - alicunde - aliqua;
- Everywhere:
  ubique (location) - *undique* (movement away).

8. Time

a) Point in time at which something happens (quando?)

- A point at which something happens is usually expressed by the simple ablative.

Aestate et potione et cibo saepius corpus eget.
During summer the body needs to drink and eat more often.

Mense malas Maio nubere vulgus ait.
People say that unlucky women marry in May.

- Dates in the Roman calendar are indicated in the following way. The Calends, the Nones and the Ides are indicated with the simple ablative (*Kalendis, Nonis, Idibus Ianuariis, Februariis, Martiis, Aprilibus, Maiis, Iuniis, Iuliis* or *Quintilibus, Augustis* or *Sextilibus, Septembribus, Octobribus, Novembribus,*

Decembribus). For other days, the date is calculated according to how many days remain to the next Calends, Nones, or Ides, including the starting and the ending day. So one day is to be added to the calculation. Then the formulae *ante diem I (II, III etc.) Kalendas (Nonas, Idus) Ianuarias (Februarias, etc.)* are used. It is to be remembered that the Calends are always the first day of the month, the Nones are the fifth day except in the months of March, May, July and October, when they are the seventh day; the Ides are the thirteenth day, except in the months of March, May, July and October, when they are the fifteenth day. The day before the Calends, Nones or Ides is expressed by *pridie* (which is an old ablative) and the accusative *Kalendas, Nonas, Idus*.

Kalendis Ianuariis
January 1

pridie Kalendas Ianuarias
December 31

a.d. XI Kalendas Maias
April 21

- In indications of age (*pueritia, adulescentia, iuventus, senectus*), offices (*consulatus, praetura, dictatura*), in using the words *adventus* and *discessus*, and also some words indicating military actions (*bellum, pugna, proelium*), we use the simple ablative if the noun in question is accompanied by an adjective, and the ablative preceded by *in* if it is used alone.

in pueritia
in childhood

prima pueritia
in early childhood

in bello
in war

bello Punico
during the Punic war

- *Hoc tempore* means "at this moment", while *in hoc tempore* means "under these circumstances, in this situation."

b) Period of time within which something happens (intra quod tempus?)

Temporal space within which something happens is usually indicated by the simple ablative.

*Roscius Romam **multis annis** non venit.*
Roscius did not come to Rome for many years.

c) Extension of time (quamdiu?)

Extension of time is expressed by the simple accusative or by the accusative preceded by the preposition *per*.

*De te **dies noctesque** cogito.*
I think of you day and night.

*Ludi **per decem dies** facti sunt.*
Public games lasting ten days have been organized.

d) General time limit (quousque?)

A general limit of time without any further indications is expressed by the accusative preceded by *(usque) ad*.

Acriter utrimque **usque ad vesperum** *pugnatum est.*
Both sides fought violently until the evening.

e) Time limit with reference to the moment of speaking (post quantum temporis?)

A time limit with reference to the moment of speaking is expressed
by the preposition *post* followed by a cardinal or ordinal number in
the accusative (the ordinal should be increased by one number, since
both the beginning and the ending units are counted).

Legati dixerunt **post tertium diem** *(=post duos dies) se reversuros
esse.*
The ambassadors said that they would be back in two days.

f) Point in time in the past with reference to the moment of speaking (quantum temporis abhinc?)

A point in time in the past with reference to the moment of speaking
is expressed in the following ways:

- when the action belongs only to the past, by a cardinal number
  in the accusative or the ablative preceded by *abhinc*;
- when the action continues until the present time, by *iam* and an
  ordinal number in the accusative, increased by one unit.

Demosthenes **abhinc annos prope trecentos** *fuit.*
Demosthenes lived almost three hundred years ago (words of Cicero).

Octavum iam annum *urbs sub hostium potestate est.*
The city has been under the dominion of the enemies for seven years.

g) Point in time in reference to another point of time (quamdiu antea? quamdiu postea?)

A point in time in reference to another point of time is expressed in the following ways: by the prepositions *ante* or *post* followed by the accusative; by the ablative followed by *ante* or *post*; by *ante* or *post* used between the words in the accusative or the ablative.

*Hoc accidit **ante** (**post**) **decem annos**.*
           ***decem annis ante** (**post**)*
           decem ante** (**post**) **annos
           decem ante** (**post**) **annis
This happened ten years earlier (later).

h) Frequency within a certain period of time (quotiens?)

The frequency of an action within a certain space of time is expressed by a numerical adverb followed by the preposition *in* and the time period in the ablative.

***Semel in anno** licet insanire.*
Once a year one is allowed to act like a madman.

i) Frequency within the course of time (quam saepe?)

The frequency within the course of time is expressed by an ordinal number, accompanied by *quisque* and the temporal substantive, all of which should be in the simple ablative. The ordinal number is usually increased by one.

***Quinto quoque anno** Sicilia tota censetur.*
Every fifth year (i.e. every four years) all Sicily is assessed.

j) *Intended point in time (ad quod tempus?)*

Intended point in time is expressed by *in* followed by the accusative.

Comitia in mensem Iulium dilata sunt.
The elections were postponed until July.

9. Instrument (quibus auxiliis?)

We express instrumentality with the simple ablative if the instrument is inanimate. If it is animate, we use the preposition *per* and the accusative.

Dente lupus, cornu taurus petit.
The wolf attacks with teeth, the bull with horns.

Imperator per legatos bella administrabat.
The commander fought the wars through deputies.

10. Manner (quomodo? qua ratione?)

Manner is expressed by the ablative preceded by the preposition *cum*. When the substantive is accompanied by an adjective, we may use either the simple ablative, or the ablative with the preposition *cum,* which in such cases is placed between the substantive and the adjective.

Cum lacrimis epistulam legit.
He read the letter with tears.

Multis lacrimis epistulam legit. =Multis cum lacrimis epistulam legit.
He read the letter with a lot of tears.

11. Accompaniment (quocum? quacum?)

Accompaniment is expressed by the preposition *cum* and the ablative.

*Nec **tecum** vivere possum, nec sine te.*
I can live neither with you nor without you.

12. Price and value (quanti?)

To express an opinion, estimate, or appraisal of the worth or value or importance of something, the genitive is used. To express the price of something that has been or might actually be bought or sold, the ablative is used - except that even where the price of something bought or sold is involved, the words *tanti, quanti, pluris* and *minoris* are used in the genitive, not the ablative.

*In rebus dubiis **plurimi** est audacia.*
Courage is very important in an uncertain situation.

***Viginti talentis** unam orationem Isocrates vendidit.*
Isocrates sold one speech of his for twenty talents.

13. Degree of difference (quanto maior? quanto melior? etc.)

Degree of difference is expressed by the simple ablative.

*Sol **multis partibus** maior quam terra universa.*
The sun is many sizes bigger than the entire earth.

14. Quality (qualis?)

Permanent physical qualities are usually expressed by the simple ablative, while moral qualities and statements of weight, number, and time are expressed by the genitive. Momentary moral qualities may be expressed by the simple ablative.

*vir **statura humili** et **corpore exiguo***
a man with an insignificant height and a small body

*vir **magni ingenii***
a man with great talents

***multorum annorum** tyrannis*
a tyranny of many years

***Bono animo** es!*
Cheer up!

15. Quantity, partition, abundance, lack (quantus? quantum? quot?)

The genitive is used after substantives indicating quantity, number, weight, and after adverbs indicating quantity. The genitive usually points to a part of a totality. The abundance or lack of something is expressed by the ablative.

*Flumina iam **lactis**, iam flumina **nectaris** ibant.*
At one time there flowed rivers of milk, at another of nectar.

*Satis **eloquentiae**, **sapientiae** parum.*
Enough eloquence, little intelligence.

*Quid **novi**? - Nihil **novi**.*
What is new? - Nothing new.

*Villa abundat **porco, haedo, agno, gallina**, **lacte, caseo, melle**.*
The country house abounds with pigs, young goats, lambs, hens, milk, cheese, and honey.

*Alter **frenis** eget, alter **calcaribus**.*
One person needs bridles, another needs spurs.

16. Cause (quare? cur? qua de causa? quam ob rem?)

Cause is expressed by the simple ablative if it is internal; by the accusative preceded by the prepositions *ob* or *propter* if it is external; by the preposition *prae* and the ablative if it is a preventing cause.

*Non dici potest quam flagrem **desiderio** Urbis.*
I cannot say how much I suffer from nostalgia for Rome.

*parere legibus **propter metum***
to obey the laws because of fear

***Prae iracundia** non sum apud me.*
I am beside myself with anger.

17. Origin (unde?)

Origin is expressed by the simple ablative or, more rarely, by the ablative preceded by the prepositions *a(ab, abs)*, *e(ex)*, or *de* if the origin is remote or if it is indicated by a pronoun.

amplissima familia *nati adulescentes*
young people born into a very important family

Ex me *atque* **ex hoc** *natus es.*
You are my son and the son of this man.

oriundi **ex Etruscis**
descended from Etruscans

18. Comparison (quo melior? qua melior? quo melius? quo maior?... inter quos maximus? inter quas maxima? inter quae maximum?...)

The person or thing used as a term of comparison in the comparative degree is expressed by the simple ablative or by *quam* and the same case as the compared person or thing. The term in the superlative degree is expressed by the genitive or by the accusative preceded by the preposition *inter.*

Res publica mihi **vitâ** *est* **meâ** *carior.* =*Res publica mihi carior est* **quam vita mea.**
My country is dearer to me than my life.

Omnium graduum *difficillimus est primus.*
The first step is most difficult of all steps.

Croesus **inter reges** *fuit opulentissimus.*
Croesus was the richest among the kings.

19. Material (qua ex re? qua de re?)

The material of which something is made is expressed by ablative preceded by the prepositions *e(ex)* or *de*.

***Ex animo** constamus et **corpore**.*
We are made up of soul and body.

*anulus **ex auro** factus*
a golden ring

20. Topic (qua de re?)

The topic or subject matter is expressed by the ablative preceded by the preposition *de*.

*Difficilis est quaestio **de natura** deorum.*
The question about the nature of deities is difficult.

21. Aim (ad quod propositum?)

We express aim by the accusative preceded by the preposition *ad*, or by the dative. Aim may also be expressed by the words *causâ* or *gratiâ* by the genitive, which have, however, a causal nuance as well.

*Dies **colloquio** dictus est.*
A day for the conference was scheduled.

*Omnia **ad bellum** parata sunt.*
Everything is ready for war.

doctor **honoris causa**
honorary doctor

22. Restriction (secundum quam rem?)

The area, field, or domain to which the action is restricted, is usually expressed by the simple ablative. If the area involved is a part of the body, then we use an accusative, called the Greek accusative. However, it is used mostly in poetry.

Doctrina *Graecia nos superabat.*
Greece was superior to us in erudition.

Glacialis hiems **canos** *hirsuta* **capillos**.
Icy winter with bristling white hair.

23. Address

To address someone, we use the vocative.

O, **di immortales**, *ubinam gentium sumus?*
O, immortal deities, where in the world are we?

Chapter VI
Word Order

1. Fundamental rules

- Word order in Latin is free, but not arbitrary. Considerations that determine it include:

  - the pragmatic function of the sentence within the discourse;
  - the emphases within the sentence;
  - the type of sentence (the sentences with the imperative, the concessive sentences and some of the interrogative sentences usually have their verb first);
  - the number of parts of the sentence and their peculiarities (e.g., the position of the verb in subjectless sentences is less fixed than in sentences with a subject);
  - elegance, rhythm, euphony (in seeking euphony, for example, we avoid putting four or five verbs together or putting words with similar endings together, especially if the endings are *-orum* or *-arum*).

- A normal word order would be as follows. The subject is in the beginning; the verbal predicate is at the end. The words that qualify the subject, i.e., adjectives, appositives, and related genitives, are located close to it. The direct object and its complements are placed after the subject. The adverbs, adverbial expressions and other complements (such as the indirect object) are positioned before the verbal predicate. If there are coordinate conjunctions (relative pronouns, temporal, causal or consecutive coordinate conjunctions) serving as a link to the preceding sentence, they are placed before the subject. However, we do not encounter this pattern very often.

Coordinate conjunction
Tum

Subject
Alexander,

Appositive to the subject
rex Macedonum,

Direct object and attribute
totam Asiam

Complement
sub potestatem suam

Verbal predicate
redegit.

Then Alexander, the king of Macedonians, took possession of all Asia.

2. Pragmatic function of the sentence within a discourse

The sentence within a discourse receives old information from the previous sentence or sentences and contains also new information of its own, which it transfers as old to the following sentence or sentences. The old information has the tendency to be placed in the beginning of the sentence, while the new information is placed toward the end. Sometimes the new information takes the first place. This is the case especially when it contrasts the old information or when an emotion is being expressed.

Ciceronis In Verrem, II, 2, 1.
Multa mihi necessario, iudices, praetermittenda sunt, ut possim aliquo

modo aliquando de his rebus quae meae fidei commissae sunt dicere (altogether new first sentence).

Recepi enim (old, introduces a sentence which will explain which things have been entrusted to Cicero) *causam Siciliae* (new)*:*

ea me ad hoc negotium (old) *provincia* (partly new, specifies the status of *Sicilia*) *attraxit* (partly new, specifies the degree of Cicero's involvement).

Ego (old) *tamen* (new, introduces a contrasting thought) *hoc* (old) *onere* (partly new, specifies the character of Cicero's commitment) *suscepto et recepta causa Siciliensi* (old) *amplexus animo* (altogether new) *sum* (old ending, refers to Cicero; otherwise new) *aliquanto amplius* (altogether new).

Suscepi enim causam (old) *totius ordinis* (altogether new), *suscepi causam* (old) *rei publicae* (altogether new), *quod putabam* (old ending, refers to Cicero; otherwise new) *tum denique recte* (new) *iudicari* (partly old, refers to *iudices* and *causa*) *posse si non modo reus improbus adduceretur, sed etiam diligens ac firmus accusator ad* (new) *iudicium* (partly old, refers to *iudices* and *causa*) *veniret* (new).

Quo (new) *mihi* (old, refers to Cicero) *maturius* (new) *ad Siciliae causam* (old) *veniendum est relictis ceteris* (new) *eius* (old, refers to *reus*) *furtis atque flagitiis, ut et viribus quam integerrimis agere et ad* (new) *dicendum* (old, refers to *causa*) *temporis satis habere possim* (old ending, refers to Cicero; otherwise new).

3. Emphasis

- The position of each word is determined by whether it is emphasized or not. The emphatic positions are the beginning and the end of the sentence. The beginning evokes the reader's interest, while the full meaning of the sentence appears at the end. The most emphasized word is located at the end of the sentence. The more unusual the position of a word, the more emphasized it is.

- To emphasize the verb, we put it at the beginning of the sentence; to emphasize the subject, we put it at the end.

***Habet** senectus magnam auctoritatem.*
Old age **does have** great authority.

*Magnam auctoritatem habet **senectus**.*
Old age has great authority.

- Any word is emphasized if it comes first or last. Of course, the subject is not emphasized if it comes first, neither is the verb emphasized if it comes last. Furthermore, if a word is separated from another word which it modifies or by which is modified, it is emphasized, especially if it also occupies first or last place in the sentence. An adjective separated from its substantive and an adverb separated from its verb are emphasized.

*Ille operam mihi dat **egregiam**.*
He takes **excellent** care of me.

*Arbores serit diligens agricola, quarum aspiciet bacam ipse **numquam**.*
The diligent farmer plants trees whose fruit he himself will **never** see.

4. Verb

The verb very often takes last place in the sentence.

*Nihil mihi **scripsisti**.*
You did not write me anything.

- Forms of the verb *esse,* however, when used as the copula (that is, merely to connect the subject with a predicate noun or adjective) rarely take last place.

*Haec res mihi **est gratissima**.*
This thing is very pleasant for me.

- If we wish to give emphasis to the verb, we put it in first place in the sentence.

***Fuit, fuit** quondam in hac re publica virtus.*
There was once, **there really was** moral perfection in this state.

- The infinitive is placed before the conjugated verb.

*Prae lacrimis plura **scribere prohibeor**.*
I am prevented from writing more because of the tears.

5. Subject

- The subject is often placed at the beginning or very close to the beginning, i.e., after a coordinate conjunction.

***Canis mortuus** non mordet.*
A dead dog does not bite.

*Signum tubae est datum. **Tum omnes** currere incipiunt.*
A trumpet signal was given. Then everybody started to run.

- The subject is not at the beginning if there is another emphasized word.

Omnia *vincit amor.*
Love conquers **all**.

6. Direct object

- The direct object is normally placed immediately after the subject.

Romulus **urbem Romam** *condidit.*
Romulus founded the city of Rome.

- The direct object takes the first place of the sentence when .emphasized.

see *5. Subject.* ***Omnia*** *vincit amor.*

7. Complements in the dative and the ablative

- Complements expressed by the dative (mainly the indirect object) and the ablative are normally placed between the subject and the verb and immediately before the word to which they are related.

Hanc epistulam ***fratri*** *misi.*
I sent this letter to my brother.

Error ***a culpa*** *vacat.*
The mistake is free of blame.

- These complements may take first or last place if they are emphasized.

Naturae omnes paremus.
All of us obey **nature**.

8. Specification in the genitive

- A specifying complement in the genitive may be placed either before or after the word to which it is related, but is most often placed before.

studiorum ardor
passion for studies

- The genitive always comes first when forming a phrase with the ablatives *causâ, gratiâ.*

doctor honoris causa
honorary doctor

- However, if the genitive is much longer than the word to which it is related, and the latter is a monosyllable, then the genitive is placed after the monosyllable.

vis cupiditatum
the force of desires

- There are some phrases with an established word order.

terrae motus
earthquake

Marci filius
son of Marcus

***Marci** nepos*
grandson of Marcus

*orbis **terrarum***
the world

*pater **familias***
the head of the household

***senatus** auctoritas*
a decree of the Senate

***senatus** consultum*
a decree of the Senate

***plebis (populi)** scitum*
a decree of the people

*magister **equitum***
the chief of the cavalry

*tribunus **militum***
a military tribune

*tribunus **plebis***
a tribune of the people

9. Adjective

- The adjective usually follows the word which it modifies. If
  we want to emphasize it, we put it before the word to which it is
  related.

vir **bonus**
a morally good man

bonus *vir*
a man with a really good soul

- Pronouns, numerals and adjectives indicating quantity usually precede the word which they modify.

haec *opinio*
this opinion

duo *consules*
two consuls

permulti *homines*
very many people

- There are some phrases with an established position of the adjective.

civis **Romanus**
a Roman citizen

ius **civile**
the civil law

aes **alienum**
a debt

bellum **civile**
a civil war

di **immortales**
immortal gods

Lar familiaris
the household hearth

Iuppiter Optimus Maximus
Jupiter, best and greatest

senatus populusque Romanus
the Roman senate and people

res familiaris
a household

- In all the phrases with *res* that form a single concept the adjective follows:

res publica
a commonwealth

res domesticae
domestic affairs

res urbanae
civil affairs

res forenses
judiciary affairs

res gestae
exploits

If the adjective and the substantive do not form one notion, the adjective usually precedes the substantive *res*:

Minimae *saepe res maiora destruunt.*
Things of very small importance often destroy bigger things.

- We may put another complement between the adjective and the modified word.

*multa tua **erga me** beneficia*
your many benefits in my favor

*filius **patri** similis*
a son similar to his father

10. Appositive

- The word in apposition usually follows the word to which it is related.

*A **littera***
the letter A

*Cicero **consul***
the consul Cicero

*Corioli **oppidum***
the town of Corioli

*ciconia, **nuntia veris***
the stork, a messenger of spring

- Some appositives come before the word to which they are related.

***urbs** Roma*
the city of Rome

imperator Caesar
the emperor Caesar

provincia Sicilia
the province of Sicily

tragoedia (fabula) Troades
the tragedy "The Trojan women"

- If we want to emphasize the appositive, we put it before the word to which it is related.

insula Lemnos
the island of Lemnos (and not the town of Lemnos)

consul Servilius
Servilius the consul (during his consulship)

11. Adverb

- An adverb usually precedes the verb or the adjective which it modifies.

*Latrones **male** vivunt.*
Bandits live bad lives.

***admodum** adulescens*
quite a young person

- A phrase equivalent to an adverb precedes the verb to which it is related.

cum virtute *vivere*
to live with virtue

- If we need to emphasize an adverb or an adverbial phrase, we place it at the beginning or at the end of the sentence.

Magis *te quam oculos meos amo.*
I love you **more** than my own eyes.

12. Coordinate conjunctions

The coordinate conjunctions *quoque, enim, autem, vero* and *igitur* do not take first place in the sentence.
The coordinate conjunctions *etiam, nam, etenim, ergo* and *itaque* take first place in the sentence.
The coordinate conjunction *tamen* may or may not take first place in the sentence.

For examples see *II. Coordinate connections.*

13. Peculiarities

- Prepositions tend to be located between the adjective and the substantive.

magno **cum** *dolore*
with great pain

paucos **post** *dies*
after a few days

*magna **ex** parte*
to a large extent

*nulla **in** re*
in nothing

*haec **de** summo malo bonoque dissensio*
this disagreement about the greatest evil and good

- The preposition *cum* is attached to certain pronouns when used with them, producing the following compounds: *mecum, tecum, secum, nobiscum, vobiscum, quocum, quacum, quibuscum.*

*Dominus **vobiscum**!*
The Lord be with you!

- *Ille* follows the word which it modifies when used to mean "famous".

*Socrates **ille***
the famous Socrates

- *Quisque* is placed after *suus* or an adjective in the superlative degree.

***Suae quisque** faber est fortunae.*
Everybody is the maker of his own fortune.

***Optimum quidque** rarissimum est.*
The best things are very rare.

- Words derived from the same root and words of the same type stay close to each other. The words *se, suus, ipse, quisque*, for example, are often used in close proximity to each other.

*Nulla **virtus virtuti** est contraria.*
No virtue is opposite to another virtue.

***Tene ego** aspicio?*
Is it you that I see?

***Aliis aliunde** est periculum.*
Risks for different people come from different sources.

***Timor timorem** pellit.*
One fear dispels another.

*Sceleris **sui sibi** conscius.*
Aware of his own crime.

*Si **quis quid** quaerat.*
If anybody were to ask anything.

- The relative and the interrogative pronouns take first place and are placed even before a preposition.

***Quem ad finem** furor iste tuus nos eludet?*
To what end will this rage of yours mislead us?

14. Order of subordinate clauses

There is no one principle for the ordering of subordinate clauses within a complex sentence. They most often occupy the position of the part of the sentence to which they logically correspond, i.e., substantive clauses occupy the position of the subject or the object, adjective clauses occupy the position of an adjective, and adverbial clauses occupy the position of an adverb. However, this is not always the case.

Furthermore, we have the rule of logical sense according to which, for example, a result clause follows the main one, or the clause with the causal *cum* precedes the main one, since it gives the motivation for its action.

In general, the subordinate clause may follow or precede the main one, it may be placed within the main one, or it may include the main one in itself, and there is no definite rule for determining its position. Usually, the narrative texts have a simpler and a clearer structure, while the oratorical texts are more complicated.

According to the research done by Nägelsbach (see the bibliography), there are four possible ways of ordering a sentence composed of one main clause (A) and one subordinate clause (a); there are five possible ways of ordering a sentence with one main clause (A) and two subordinate clauses independent of each other (a) and (b). There are more possible ways of sentence-ordering when the main clause (A) has a subordinate clause of the first degree (a) on which a subordinate clause of the second degree (α) depends. Obviously, it becomes much more complicated when there are other subordinate clauses of first, second, etc., degrees.

- Architectonics of one main and one subordinate clause.

a : A	*Ut me in angustiis adiuves a te quaero.*
A (a) A	*A te ut me in angustiis adiuves quaero.*
A / a	*A te quaero ut me in angustiis adiuves.*
a (A) a	*In angustiis a te quaero ut me adiuves.*

I ask you to help me in my difficulties.

- Architectonics of one main and two subordinate independent clauses.

a : A / b	*Cum auxilio egerem, a te statim petivi ut mihi subvenires.*
a : A (b) A	*Cum auxilio egerem, a te ut mihi subvenires statim petivi.*

113

A (a) A / b   *A te ut mihi subvenires statim petivi, cum auxilio egerem.*

A (a) A (b) A   *A te ut mihi subvenires statim, cum auxilio egerem, petivi.*

a : b : A   *Cum auxilio egerem, ut mihi subvenires a te statim petivi.*

Since I needed help, I immediately asked you to come and help me.

- Architectonics of one main clause, one subordinate clause of first degree, and another subordinate clause of second degree. We indicate only several possibilities.

a (α) a : A   *Cum quid faciendum esset nescirem, a te consilium petivi.*

a / α : A   *Cum nescirem quid faciendum esset, a te consilium petivi.*

A (a [α] a) A   *A te, cum quid faciendum esset nescirem, consilium petivi.*

A (a / α) A   *A te, cum nescirem quid faciendum esset, consilium petivi.*

A / a (α) a   *A te consilium petivi, cum quid faciendum esset nescirem.*

α : a : A   *Quid faciendum esset cum nescirem, a te consilium petivi.*

A (α : a) A   *A te, quid faciendum esset cum nescirem, consilium petivi.*

A / α : a   *A te consilium petivi, quid faciendum esset cum nescirem.*

I asked you for advice because I did not know what was to be done.

Chapter VII
The Use of Vocabulary in Latin Composition

In writing in Latin today, we first of all need to preserve the genuine structure of the language. Latin certainly went through many transformations at various periods, as well as through differences of style in different authors. In Seneca we already find the first signs of the dominance of parataxis (simple sentences without subordination). The Bible and many Christian writers adhere to a paratactic structure as well. Other writers, however, follow the models of the classical hypotactic syntax (abundance of subordination). The latter is particularly dear to the humanists. Both hypotaxis and parataxis may be used in composition today; the choice will depend on the literary genre and the style we want to use. A more paratactic structure does not necessarily mean a less Latin one. However, the rules of genuine Latinity are always to be observed. Such rules apply to the expression of relations through cases, not through prepositions or word order; the use of accusative with infinitive and not the use of a clause with *quod* or *quoniam* for an indirect statement; the correct use of the subjunctive, etc. Certain rules need to be observed since, once the fundamental structure of the language has been compromised, it is no longer the same language.

As far as lexical innovations are concerned, however, we have much greater freedom. Even the classical authors encourage us in this respect. Cicero, who sometimes himself creates new words (cf. the famous *sullaturit* and *proscripturit*) in order to be more expressive, says: "*sunt rebus novis nova ponenda nomina*" (*De natura deorum, 1, 44*). Horace in *Ars poetica, 58-59* grants to posterity the right to create neologisms: *"Licuit semperque licebit signatum praesente nota producere nomen."* Quintilian, the authoritative expert on style is clear in *Institutiones oratoriae, VIII, c.3*: *"Audendum itaque. Neque enim accedo Celso, qui ab oratore verba fingi vetat."* The first Christians had to express concepts which had not been known earlier. So they borrowed words from Hebrew (for example, *amen, alleluia*), from Greek (for example, *episcopus, apostolus*); they changed the meaning of some words which already existed in Latin (for example *oro, paganus, Dominus*), and they created neologisms (for example *Salvator, incarnatio*). Tertullian himself created more than 900 neologisms, although not more than 300 of them remained in use after him. Thus, the persistence of some *Ciceroniani* in reducing latinity only to Cicero's vocabulary, an approach disapproved by Cicero himself, does not seem appropriate. Concepts belonging to different times and different fields can be expressed in Latin with equal success. It is possible also, when necessary, to borrow from Greek, as the Romans did themselves. Certainly, however, in creating new words in Latin, we need to follow the genuine Latin word structure.

Which dictionaries are to be used in Latin composition? Appropriate are not only dictionaries containing entries in modern languages, with Latin translations, but also classical dictionaries of Latin and synonym dictionaries.

The most important dictionaries with modern-language entries and Latin translations are the following: H. **Goelzer**, E. **Benoist**, *Nouveau dictionnaire français-latin*, Paris 1892 (1936[6]), the best dictionary from a modern language into Latin; L. **Quicherat**, É. **Chatelain**, *Dictionnaire français-latin*, Paris, 1847 (reprinted 1952); O. **Badellino**, *Dizionario italiano-latino*, Torino 1961 (reprinted 1972), sometimes quite vague; A. **Perugini**, *Dizionario italiano-latino*, Roma 1976, providing many terms used by the Roman Curia, full of Italianisms, which defect, however, is compensated for by the inclusion of many synonyms. The best dictionary from English into Latin is W. **Smith**, T.D. Hall, *A Copious and Critical English-Latin Dictionary*, New York 1871.

Consulting a Greek-Latin dictionary can also be useful in composition. Such a dictionary is: E.F. **Leopold**, *Lexicon Graeco-Latinum manuale*, Lipsiae 1830 (1852^2, reprinted 1992).

Some dictionaries aim at gathering modern concepts, concepts that did not exist in the ancient world, or terms used more frequently today than in ancient Latin texts, on account of the literary character of the latter. These dictionaries include: A. **Bacci**, *Lexicon eorum vocabulorum quae difficilius Latine redduntur*, Roma 1963, which often provides Latin descriptions or paraphrases rather than actual translations; C. **Egger**, *Lexicon recentis Latinitatis,* Roma 1992-1997, in two volumes (a third volume with addenda is forthcoming); C. **Helfer**, *Lexicon auxiliare. Ein deutsch-lateinisches Wörterbuch*, Saarbrücken 1991; C. **Eichenseer**, *Latinitas viva*, pars lexicalis, Saraviponti 1982; idem, *Latinitas viva*, tabulae imagineae numero nonaginta, Saraviponti 1984 (the latter volume provides illustrations for the former).

Latin personal names and geographical names are easily found in the following two volumes: C. **Egger**, *Lexicon nominum virorum et mulierum*, Roma 1963; C. **Egger**, *Lexicon nominum locorum*, Roma 1977. More Latin geographical names are to be found in: J.G.T. **Grässe**, *Orbis Latinus: Lexikon lateinischer geographischer Namen*, Braunschweig 1861 (1980^2).

None of the above mentioned dictionaries is a sufficient lexical instrument for Latin composition. Above all, we need to use the classical dictionaries of Latin, which contain Latin entries with definitions in a modern language (or in Latin itself), since those dictionaries provide important information on the use of Latin words. These dictionaries include: *Thesaurus linguae Latinae*, Lipsiae 1900 ff., which is the most detailed Latin dictionary (Latin-Latin), which at present is complete only up to the letter P̱; E. **Forcellini**, *Totius Latinitatis lexicon*, Paduae 1771 (1805^2; 1827-31^3 cur. G. Furlanetto; 1864-87^4 cur. F. Corradini with 2 volumes *Onomasticon*, cur. G. Perin; 1911-20^3; 1940^5, 6 voll.; reprinted Bologna 1965) (Latin - Latin and Italian), from which the elegant C.T. **Lewis**, C. **Short**, *A Latin*

Dictionary, Oxford 1879 (reprinted 1980), rich in synonyms and antonyms, and K.E. **Georges**, *Ausführliches Lateinisch-Deutsches Handwörterbuch*, Leipzig 1837-38 (Darmstadt 1988[15]) are derived; the latter two dictionaries, however, as well as *Forcellini* itself, are obsolescent since they are based on old editions and on old readings. A new dictionary, based on new excerpts from new editions, is P.G.W. Glare, *Oxford Latin Dictionary*, Oxford 1968-82, which, however, excludes the texts after the second century A.D. and all Christian texts. A supplement to it for the remaining centuries of antiquity is provided by the dictionary of A. **Souter**, *A Glossary of Later Latin to 600 A.D.*, Oxford 1949, and for the Christian writers by A. **Blaise**, *Dictionnaire latin-français des auteurs chrétiens*, Strasbourg 1954 (Turnhout 1967). Medieval and Christian words are to be found in several medieval dictionaries, the largest of which is: **Du Cange**, *Glossarium ad scriptores mediae et infimae Latinitatis*, Niort 1883-87 (reprinted Graz 1957), though hard to use and based on old editions; J.F. **Niermeyer**, *Mediae Latinitatis lexicon minus*, Leiden 1976, an updated and condensed *Du Cange*, but like its predecessor focussed on the administrative sphere; F. **Blatt**, *Novum glossarium ad scriptores mediae Latinitatis ab anno DCCC usque ad annum MCC*, Hafniae 1957ff., which aims to be the new *Du Cange*, but for the moment covering only words from L to P; A. **Blaise**, *Lexicon Latinitatis Medii Aevi, praesertim ad res ecclesiasticas investigandas pertinens*, Turnholti 1975, relevant for philosophy, theology, canonic law, liturgy, and ecclesiastical history.

Dictionaries of synonyms may be of great use in composition. Such dictionaries include: F. **Schultz**, *Lateinische Synonymik*, Paderborn 1841 (1887[2]); E. **Barrault**, *Traité des synonymes de la langue latine*, Paris 1853; H. **Menge**, *Lateinische Synonymik*, Heidelberg, cur. O. Schönberger, 1874 (1959[5], 1988); ***Döderlein's Handbook of Latin Synonymes***, transl. from German H.H. Arnold, Andover, Mass. 1978; **Ramshorn** L., *Dictionary of Latin Synonymes*, transl. from German F. Lieber, Philadelphia 1860.

Chapter VIII
Punctuation

Since the use of punctuation differs considerably with periods and authors, we will give only a few practical rules for its use without entering into any theoretical or historical questions. Here are, in general, the rules followed by modern editors of Latin texts and by those who write in Latin today.

1. Syllable division

- When the syllable vowel is followed by the vowel of the next syllable or by only one consonant, the syllable division comes after the vowel: *le-o; ma-ter.*

- When the syllable vowel is followed by two consonants or by a double consonant, the syllable division normally comes after the first consonant: *mag-nus, ag-ger.*

- However, when the syllable vowel is followed by a combination of a mute and a liquid, the syllable division comes before these consonants: *a-trox; locu-ples.*
(Mute are the labials *p, b, ph*, the dentals *t, d, th* and the gutturals *c, g, ch*; liquid are *r* and *l*).

- When the syllable vowel is followed by three consonants, the syllable division comes after the first two: *dex-ter; ins-tar.*

- When the syllable vowel is followed by three consonants, the two latter of which are a combination of a mute and a liquid, the syllable division comes after the first consonant: *spec-trum; tem-plum.*

- In compound words the syllable division is made according to etymology: *prod-eo; ab-ripio.*

- After the fourth century the syllable division could be made anywhere, if there exists a word in Latin that begins with the same combination of letters after the division: *a-sper* (cf. *spica*), *ca-stra* (cf. *strages*), *pu-gna* (cf. *gnarus*).

2. Punctuation marks

The function of punctuation marks is to help the reader in understanding the text by indicating short and long logical pauses. In this sense their use is quite free.

a) Comma

The comma separates different elements of the same clause.

- We use a comma to separate elements of the clause which are in the same syntactic position.

Ex cupiditatibus odia, discidia, discordiae, seditiones, bella nascuntur.
Hatred, disagreements, discords, quarrels, wars are born from cupidities.

- The vocative case is separated by a comma from the rest of the phrase.

O rus, quando ego te aspiciam?
O countryside, when will I see you?

- The appositive is separated from the rest of the sentence by a comma.

Historia, magistra vitae, immortalitati commendatur.
History, the teacher of life, is entrusted to immortality.

A comma separates clauses in a complex sentence. The rules for this separation are more descriptive than prescriptive, and the use is different in different editions.

- Coordinate clauses are usually not separated by a comma except when there is an asyndeton. The comma often precedes adversative clauses with *autem* or *vero* in second position.

Dominus dedit, Dominus abstulit.
The Lord granted, the Lord took away.

Ipse nihil scribo, lego autem libentissime.
I do not write anything, but I read very willingly.

- Substantive complementary clauses are usually not separated by a comma because, logically, they are usually a subject or an object.

- Relative clauses are usually not separated by a comma if they follow the main clause. If, however, they precede the main clause, they are usually separated from it by a comma.

Quod non dedit fortuna, non eripit.
Fortune does not take away what it has not given.

- Adverbial clauses (only the explicit ones) tend to be separated by a comma from the main sentence both when they precede it and when they follow it.

Si peccavi, insciens feci.
If I made a mistake, I made it unawares.

Spero me sic vivere, ut nemini iocus sim.
I hope I live so as not to be an object of derision for anybody.

- Subordinate sentences that are situated within the main clause are separated from it by a comma.

Cura, quod potes, ut valeas.
Take care to be well, as far as you can.

- A comma may be placed wherever the sense requires, especially in long and complex sentences.

Efferor studio patres vestros, quos colui et dilexi, videndi, neque vero eos solos convenire aveo, quos ipse cognovi, sed illos etiam de quibus audivi et legi et ipse conscripsi.
I am exalted by the eagerness to see your fathers, whom I respected and loved, and I yearn to meet not only these whom I knew myself, but also those of whom I have heard and read and written.

b) Period

We use a period at the end of the declarative sentences.

Finis coronat opus.
The end crowns the work.

Non novi vos.
I do not know you.

Hoc quaerat aliquis.
Somebody might ask that.

Sine te non viverem.
I would not live without you.

c) Question mark

We use a question mark at the end of the interrogative sentences.

Quid est veritas?
What is the truth?

Quid faciam? Quo me vertam?
What should I do? Where should I turn?

d) Exclamation mark

We use an exclamation mark at the end of the imperative and exclamatory sentences.

Sequere me!
Follow me!

Noli me tangere!
Do not touch me!

Guadeamus igitur!
Let us then rejoice!

Soli Deo gloria!
Glory only for God!

O tempora, o mores!
O times, o morals!

e) Semicolon

The semicolon signals a longer pause than the comma and a shorter one than the period. We use a semicolon when the sense of two clauses is not thoroughly complete by itself. We use it also between very short or contradictory clauses.

Si vales, bene est; ego valeo.
If you are well, that is fine; I am well.

Funus interim procedit: sequimur; ad sepulcrum venimus; in ignem imposita est; fletur.
In the meantime the funeral procession goes on; we arrive at the burial-place; the dead woman has been laid on the fire; everybody weeps.

f) Colon

We use a colon before the beginning of direct speech, before explaining or accounting for something mentioned previously, or before indicating the consequence of the previous clause.

Convivae dicunt: vivamus, moriendum est.
The table-companions say: let us live, we will have to die.

Efficit hoc philosophia: medetur animis.
Philosophy has the following effect: it heals souls.

g) *Ellipsis points*

Ellipsis points are used to suspend the thought in an indefinite way, leaving something to be guessed at. They often express the author's emotion or some ironic nuance.

Quos ego . . . sed motos praestat componere fluctus.
Whom should I . . . but it is better to calm down the violent waves.

h) *Quotation marks*

We put in quotation marks the direct speech or single quoted words.

Scipio Africanus turpe esse aiebat in re militari dicere: "non putaram".
Scipio Africanus used to say that it is a shame to say in military action: "I haven't thought about that."

Diu est "iam" id mihi.
This "right now" is too long for me.

i) *Dash*

We use the dash to introduce a phrase or clause not syntactically a part of the larger sentence.

Sine amicitia igitur – omnes hoc consentiunt – nulla vita esse potest.
Therefore, without friendship – everybody agrees on that – there cannot be any life.

j) Parentheses

The use of parentheses is similar to that of the dash. They enclose a parenthetical thought, that is, an explanation or an inserted clause, without interrupting the thought of the main sentence.

Precor ut quandoque veniat dies (utinamque iam venerit!).
I pray that this day arrive sometime (I wish that it had already arrived!).

k) Dieresis.

We use dieresis to indicate that the vowels in the diphthongs *oe* and *ae* should be read separately. However, the dieresis is often omitted in editions.

poëta
a poet

aër
air

l) Signs of vowel length

The signs of vowel length are usually not present in the editions of Latin texts, but they may be of some use in texts intended for students.

Vocāles correptas et productas oportet sedŭle distinguāmus.
We need to distinguish diligently between short and long vowels.

3. Some orthographical questions

a) Capital letters

- Personal and geographic names and the substantives and adjectives derived from them are written with a capital letter: *Latinitas, Christianus*.

- Names of months and of athletic competitions are also written with a capital letter: *Ianuarius; Olympia*.

- In some editions, sentences begin with a capital letter only at the beginning of a new paragraph.

b) J and V/U

- The letter *J, j* is usually avoided in indicating the semivowel *i* (between two vowels or at the beginning of the word before a vowel) because it is a late invention. In its place, the letter *I, i* is usually used.

- The ancient Romans used the letter *V, u* to indicate both the vowel and the semivowel. However, on account of a strong tradition, we often use *U, u* to indicate the vowel and *V, v* to indicate the semivowel.

c) Italics

Italics may be used instead of quotation marks.

Chapter IX
Reworking Texts

In reworking texts, we do not compose freely but rewrite already existing Latin writings. We may rework texts by asking questions and then answering them; by making a summary of the text and trying to find a good Latin title for it; by simplifying compound complex sentences into simple sentences or vice versa; by explaining the text in Latin using synonyms and different grammatical constructions; by rendering an implicit dialogue explicit; by converting poetic language into prose etc. Below are some examples of such reworking.

1. Asking Latin questions and answering them

Ciceronis Ad familiares, 14, 12

Tullius Terentiae suae s.d.
Quod nos in Italiam salvos venisse gaudes, perpetuo gaudeas velim. Sed perturbati dolore animi magnisque iniuriis metuo ne id consilii ceperimus quod non facile explicare possimus. Qua re, quantum potes adiuva; quid autem possis mihi in mentem non venit. In viam quod te des hoc tempore nihil est. Et longum est iter et non tutum; et non video quid prodesse possis si veneris.
Vale.

D. pr. Non. Nov. Brundisio.

Quis has litteras scribit? - Marcus Tullius Cicero scribit. Ille est huius epistulae auctor.

Cui misit epistulam? Ad quem eam direxit? - Terentiae, uxori suae, Cicero epistulam misit.

Ubi versatur Cicero? Unde dedit epistulam?- Cicero Brundisii versatur. Brundisium est portus in Apulia, in Italia scilicet meridiana. Ergo Cicero Brundisio epistulam dedit.

Quando data est epistula? - Epistula pridie Nonas Novembres data est, id est die quarto mensis Novembris.

Quo animo scribit Cicero? - Perturbatus scribit, confusus atque sollicitus. Et ipse dolet, et familiares eius iniuriis et contumeliis sunt affecti.

Sed quid factum est? - Cicero peregrinatus erat. Deinde in Italiam revertit et Terentiae quae forsitan Romae est, scripsit se salvum pervenisse. Terentia rescripsit se gaudere quod maritus salvus in Italiam pervenit. Cicero autem ironice ei rescribit se velle eam perpetuo gaudere, quod tamen vix fieri potest. Nam Cicero haud bonum consilium cepit, quia id efficere non potest. Melius fortasse esset ab Italia abesse.

Quid Cicero a Terentia petit? - Cicero a Terentia auxilium petit.

Quod auxilium accuratius Cicero requirit? - Nil certi Cicero a Terentia petit. Vult enim eam auxilium ferre, sed quod auxilium sit ferendum nescit.

Oportetne Terentia Brundisium petere? - Minime.

Qua de causa Brundisium non est Terentiae petendum? - Tres sunt huius rei causae. Primum, iter satis longum est. Secundum, iter plenum est periculorum. Tertium, etiam si venerit, Terentia utilitatis sit nullius.

2. Making a summary in Latin and finding a Latin title

Senecae Consolatio ad Marciam, 19, 5

Mors dolorum omnium exsolutio est et finis ultra quem mala nostra non exeunt, quae nos in illam tranquillitatem in qua antequam iacuimus reponit. Si mortuorum aliquis misereretur, et non natorum misereatur. Mors nec bonum nec malum est; id enim potest aut bonum aut malum esse quod aliquid est; quod vero ipsum nihil est et omnia in nihilum redigit, nulli nos fortunae tradit. Mala enim bonaque circa aliquam versantur materiam: non potest id fortuna tenere quod natura dimisit, nec potest miser esse qui nullus est.

De morte non metuenda (vel Mortem non esse metuendam)

Mors omnium malorum finis est. Itaque mors tranquillitas est. Mortui et non nati eodem modo se habent. Substantia mortis nihil exstat. Si nihil est, mors nec bona nec mala est. Si mors mala non est, metuenda non videtur nec oportet mortuorum misereamur.

3. Changing a compound complex sentence into simple sentences

Livii Ab Urbe condita, XXI, I.

I. In parte operis mei licet mihi praefari, quod in principio summae totius professi plerique sunt rerum scriptores, bellum maxime omnium memorabile, quae umquam gesta sint, me scripturum, quod Hannibale duce Carthaginienses cum populo Romano gessere. Nam neque validiores opibus ullae inter se civitates gentesque contulerunt arma neque his ipsis tantum umquam virium aut roboris fuit, et haud ignotas belli artes inter sese sed expertas primo Punico conferebant bello, et adeo varia fortuna belli ancepsque Mars fuit, ut propius periculum fuerint qui vicerunt. Odiis etiam prope maioribus certarunt quam viribus, Romanis indignantibus quod victoribus victi ultro inferrent arma, Poenis quod superbe avareque crederent imperitatum victis esse. Fama est etiam Hannibalem annorum ferme novem pueriliter *blandientem patri Hamilcari, ut duceretur in Hispaniam, cum perfecto Africo bello exercitum eo traiecturus sacrificaret, altaribus admotum tactis sacris iure iurando adactum, se cum primum posset hostem fore populo Romano.*

In this passage, there are four compound complex sentences, which can be transformed into more than twenty-five simple sentences.

Plerique rerum scriptores in principio summae totius aliqua profitentur. Licet autem mihi medio in opere prooemium exarare. Bellum scripturus sum. Quod bellum Hannibale duce Carthaginienses cum populo Romano gessere. Idem maxime est memorabile omnium rerum gestarum. Nam nullae validiores opibus inter se civitates gentesque contulerunt arma. His ipsis quoque numquam tantum virium aut roboris fuit. Nec ignotas belli artes inter sese sed expertas primo Punico conferebant bello. Fortuna belli valde varia fuit et Mars anceps. Quapropter victores propius periculum fuerunt. Odiis etiam prope maioribus certarunt quam viribus. Nam Romani indignabantur. Victi enim sententia Romanorum victoribus ultro inferebant arma. Poeni quoque indignabantur. "Superbe avareque victis est imperitatum" dicebant. Porro fama tenet haec. Hannibal annorum ferme novem natus erat. Pater eius Hamilcar Africum bellum perfecerat. Exercitum in Hispaniam erat traiecturus. Ante profectum vero sacrificabat. Hannibal patri blandiri coepit. Cupiebat enim in Hispaniam duci. Tunc pater eum altaribus admovit. Dein sacra tangere coegit. Denique filium iure iurando coegit. Ius autem iurandum hoc erat: "Quam primum hostis fiam populi Romani."

4. Explaining a text in Latin using synonyms

Taciti Annales, XV, 38

38.1. Sequitur clades, forte an dolo principis incertum - nam utrumque auctores prodidere -, sed omnibus quae huic Urbi per violentiam ignium acciderunt gravior atque atrocior.

Successit (postea accidit) calamitas (malum). Dubium est (ambiguum est, nescimus) utrum casu (fortuito, fortuna, temere) acciderit an fraude (fallacia, astutia) imperatoris. Nam scriptores utramque rem narraverunt. Omnium tamen incendiorum quae Romae evenerunt maximum fuit atque ferocissimum.

2. Initium in ea parte circi ortum quae Palatino Caelioque montibus contigua est, ubi per tabernas, quibus id mercimonium inerat quo flamma alitur, simul coeptus ignis et statim validus et vento citus longitudinem circi corripuit; neque enim domus munimentis saeptae vel templa muris cincta aut quid aliud morae interiacebat.

Incendium incepit in ea parte circi quae proxima (vicina) est Palatino et Caelio montibus. Illic exstabant officinae, in quibus inveniebantur merces aptae (faciles) ad comburendum. Ibi ignis incepit et eo ipso tempore iam fortis factus est et velox (rapidus) propter ventum. Totum circum cepit. Nam liberum erat spatium (nihil obstaculi erat), nec aedificia parietibus circumdata, nec fana maceriis vallata.

3. Impetu pervagatum, incendium plana primum, deinde in edita adsurgens et rursus

Incendium vehementer erravit (palatum est). Primo campos (planitiem) devastavit, deinde inferiora populando, anteiit remedia velocitate mali et obnoxia Urbe artis itineribus hucque et illuc flexis atque enormibus vicis, qualis vetus Roma fuit.

ascendit in colles (in loca excelsa, loca alta) et iterum in planitiem descendit. Ergo velocius fuit remediis propter duas causas: ipse ignis celer (velox, citus, rapidus) erat; urbs quoque subdita (subiecta) erat igni propter angustas vias et partes urbis tortuosas et sine regulis. Talis fuit antiqua Roma.

4. Ad hoc lamenta paventium feminarum, fessa aetate aut rudis pueritiae, quique sibi quique aliis consulebant, dum trahunt invalidos aut opperiuntur, pars mora, pars festinans, cuncta impediebant.

Ad hoc addebatur (accedebat) quod questus (ploratus, fletus, ululatus, gemitus) metuentium mulierum, vel anuum vel puellarum, et alii qui se ipsos vel ceteros curabant, dum imbecillos (saucios, debiles, infirmos) ducunt (tractant, rapiunt) vel exspectant (praestolantur), pars tardantes, pars festinatione, omnibus obstaculum erant (obsistebant, omnia interpellabant, remorabantur).

5. Et saepe, dum in tergum respectant, lateribus aut fronte circumveniebantur; vel, si in proxima evaserant, illis quoque igni correptis, etiam quae longinqua crediderant in eodem casu reperiebant.

Et haud raro, dum rursus inspiciunt, dextra et laeva et ante faciem igni circumscribuntur. Vel si in vicinia (in vicina, in vicinitatem) aufugerant, etiam loca longe distantia igni capta reperiebant.

6. Postremo, quid vitarent, quid peterent ambigui, complere vias, sterni per agros; quidam, amissis omnibus fortunis, diurni quoque victus, alii caritate suorum, quos eripere nequiverant, quamvis patente effugio, interiere.

Denique nesciebant unde fugerent, quo irent. Replebant enim itinera, se prosternebant (se profligebant) per campos. Nonnulli, cum omnia bona perdidissent, etiam panem cottidianum, alii propter desiderium (amorem) familiarium mortuorum quos educere non potuerant, mortui sunt (animam exspiraverunt, animam egerunt, mortem obiverunt, diem supremum obiverunt, mortem occubuerunt, perierunt, occiderunt), quamquam effugere licebat (licet effugium pateret).

7. Nec quisquam defendere audebat, crebris multorum minis restinguere prohibentium, et quia alii palam faces iaciebant atque esse sibi auctorem vociferabantur, sive ut raptus licentius exercerent, seu iussu.

Nemo quoque auxilium praebere (propugnare, servare) temptabat (conabatur, moliebatur, periclitabatur) propter frequentes minas eorum qui vetabant exstinguere ignem (propter terrentes et minantes: "Ne flammas restinxeritis!"). Alii etiam aperte taedas iaciebant et dicebant sibi esse auctoritatem. Hoc faciebant sive ut liberius furarentur (raperent), sive propterea quod princeps eis hoc iusserat.

5. Rendering an implicit dialogue explicit

Martialis, VII, 3

Cur non mitto meos tibi, Pontiliane, libellos?
Ne mihi tu mittas, Pontiliane, tuos!

A dialogue developed from the implicit dialogue in the epigram.

Pontilianus: *Velim, mi Martialis, versiculos tuos legere. Nihil umquam*
ad me misisti. Quidni libellos tuos mihi muneri mittas?
Martialis: *Numquam meos libellos tibi misi, quia nolebam legere tuos.*
Nam si meos tibi dedissem, tuos statim mihi praebuisses. At poeta es
rudis nec in scriptis insulsis legendis diem terere iuvat.
Pontilianus: *Quam durus iudex videris!*

Martialis, XI, 67

Nil mihi das vivus; dicis post fata daturum.
Si non es stultus, scis, Maro, quid cupiam!

A dialogue developed from an implicit dialogue in the epigram.

Martialis: *Licetne parvulam stipem a te, optime Maro, petere? Vir*
enim bene nummatus mihi aliquam concedere poteris.
Maro: *Ne unam quidem libellam tibi decoctori dabo. Pecuniam meam*
usque ad mortem in argentaria taberna servabo. Tum hereditas tibi
testamento veniet.
Martialis: *Ergo cupio ut quam primum mortem obeas.*
Maro: *Cum hoc dicas, inter heredes non connumeraberis.*

6. Converting poetic language into prose

Catullus' description of the symptoms of being in love.
Catullus, 51, 9-12
lingua sed torpet, tenuis sub artus
flamma demanat, sonitu suopte
tintinant aures, gemina teguntur lumina nocte.

Lingua mea est languida, qua de causa loqui non licet. Corpus calidum est atque febri laboro. Porro aures munere suo non funguntur. Nam sonitus potius internos audio quam externos. Nec oculi inspicere valent. Omnia ante me obscura videntur.

Chapter X
Free Composition

In order to compose freely, we first need to find a topic. A free composition may be a narration of historical facts, a character portrayal, a moral or philosophical treatise, an accusatory or a defensive speech, an autobiographical piece, a letter, etc. For each topic, we need to find the necessary material (*inventio*, according to the vocabulary of ancient rhetoric) and to arrange it properly (*dispositio*).

The composition may have four parts: beginning (*initium* or *exordium*), link between the beginning and the exposition (*prosecutio*), exposition (*narratio* or *tractatio*) and end (*finis* or *conclusio*). We may begin in a variety of ways: from the real beginning, the middle, or the end of the topic under consideration; from a general consideration relating to the beginning, the middle, or the end of the topic; from an example relating to the beginning, the middle, or the end of the topic. The way we begin will determine the way we go on; there is a link between the beginning and the exposition. The story goes forward if we start from the very beginning, or it goes backward in other cases; it can proceed from a general consideration to concrete facts, or it can follow an analogy from an example in the beginning to what follows. In the course of the exposition, we should try to arrange the material in both directions (*in utramque partem*) if there are two different points of view, and to enrich the exposition with descriptions and poetic digressions if required by the topic. The material should be lengthened or shortened according to its nature. At the end, we should conclude with the final episode of the narrative, or with a general consideration (shifting from concrete to abstract), or with an example (analogously moving from concrete to concrete or from abstract to concrete).

1. Narration of historical facts.

We have several models of historical narration: Caesar, marked by the scrupulousness and simplicity of a chronicler, characterized by purity of language and simplicity of word choice; Livy, patriotically painting a monumental historical tableau of Roman glory, using complex and harmonious language, with compound sentences so complicated as to seem intended to be read rather than heard; Sallust, pithy and fast-moving, who uses an archaizing Latin in his denunciation of the degeneracy of contemporary Roman society; Tacitus, with his vehement style, dense, concise, and asymmetric, bitterly stating the limitations of historical progress.

The events find their place in the middle of the composition. They need to be rendered with vivacity and a clear sense of chronological order.

Possible topics: *De bello civili Americano; De Foedere Posdamensi; De pyrobolo atomico Hirosimae iniecto; De pervestigatione humana astronautica; De muro Berolinensi everso.*

Example from *Taciti Annales, lib. XVI, XV-XVI*

15. 1. Ostorius longinquis in agris, apud finem Ligurum, id temporis erat. Eo missus centurio, qui caedem eius maturaret. Causa festinandi ex eo oriebatur quod Ostorius, multa militari fama et civicam coronam apud Britanniam meritus, ingenti corporis robore armorumque scientia metum Neroni fecerat, ne invaderet pavidum semper et reperta nuper coniuratione magis exterritum. 2. Igitur centurio, ubi effugia villae clausit, iussa imperatoris Ostorio aperit. Is fortitudinem saepe adversum hostis spectatam in se vertit; et, quia venae, quamquam interruptae, parum sanguinis effundebant, hactenus manu servi usus ut immotum pugionem extolleret, adpressit dextram eius iuguloque occurrit.

16. 1. Etiam si bella externa et obitas pro re publica mortes tanta casuum similitudine memorarem, meque ipsum satias cepisset aliorumque taedium expectarem, quamvis honestos civium exitus, tristes tamen et continuos aspernantium; at nunc patientia servilis tantumque sanguinis domi perditum fatigant animum et maestitia restringunt. 2. Neque aliam defensionem ab iis quibus ista noscentur exegerim, quam ne oderim tam segniter pereuntis. Ira illa numinum in res Romanas fuit, quam non, ut in cladibus exercituum aut captivitate urbium, semel edito, transire licet. Detur hoc inlustrium virorum posteritati ut, quo modo exsequiis a promisca sepultura separantur, ita in traditione supremorum accipiant habeantque propriam memoriam.

Example of a modern historical narration written in Tacitus' style.

Saevitia Stalinii in populum Russum

Plene rerum potitus Stalinius vehementer saeviit. Quo crudelior ferociorque dictator exstitit nemo; quippe ceteris in alienos invehentibus concives delere conatus. Terram agricolis ademit officinarum operariis facilius imperaturus. Annonae caritatem inediamque molitus ineffabilem effecit ut matres fame in Ucraina confectae comederent prolem. Omnes suspectos alios ultro aliis calumnias instruentes habuit. Proditionis insimulatus dictatori proximus quisque capite multatus nec carneficibus mors pepercit. Stalinii ministri tricies centena milia, ut ferunt, in vinculis necavere nonnullis excruciatu absumptis. Periit flos ad supplicium imprimis requisitus. Nec quisquam contra dictatorem verbum proferre ausus. Post bellum Germanicum immo auctoritas tyranni crevit apud credentes eiusdem gratia Russos vicisse; ideo licuit ut vehementius saeviret. Nullum ius, nullum praesidium inermibus uniusque impunitati expositis reservatum. Ipsaeque victimae credere boni communis causa interfici. Quae ad mortem dictatoris stetere atque inter ipsas exsequias comitantes cernebantur qui obitum venerati plorarent.

2. Character portrayal

In the description of persons, we may follow the simple and clear biographies of Cornelius Nepos, the monumental portraits of Livy, the prosopographical characterizations of Sallust, the virtual *laudatio funebris* which Tacitus wrote for Agricola.
We need to concentrate on the means of indicating physical and moral qualities. These descriptions may apply to both admirable and infamous historical figure.

Possible persons to be described: *De Matre Teresia; De Sigismundo Freud; De Ioanne Paulo Sartre; De Beniamino Franklin; De Georgio Washington.*

Example from *Livii Ab Urbe condita, XXI, 4 (descriptio Hannibalis)*

4. *...Numquam ingenium idem ad res diversissimas, parendum atque imperandum, habilius fuit. Itaque haud facile discerneres, utrum imperatori an exercitui carior esset: neque Hasdrubal alium quemquam praeficere malle, ubi quid fortiter ac strenue agendum esset, neque milites alio duce plus confidere aut audere. Plurimum audaciae ad pericula capessenda, plurimum consilii inter ipsa pericula erat. Nullo labore aut corpus fatigari aut animus vinci poterat. Caloris ac frigoris patientia par; cibi potionisque desiderio naturali, non voluptate modus finitus; vigiliarum somnique nec die nec nocte discriminata tempora; id, quod gerendis rebus superesset, quieti datum; ea neque molli strato neque silentio accersita; multi saepe militari sagulo opertum humi iacentem inter custodias stationesque militum conspexerunt. Vestitus nihil inter aequales excellens: arma atque equi conspiciebantur. Equitum peditumque idem longe primus erat; princeps in proelium ibat, ultimus conserto proelio excedebat. Has tantas viri virtutes ingentia vitia aequabant: inhumana crudelitas, perfidia plus quam Punica, nihil veri, nihil sancti, nullus deum metus, nullum ius iurandum, nulla religio. Cum*

hac indole virtutum atque vitiorum triennio sub Hasdrubale imperatore meruit, nulla re quae agenda videndaque magno futuro duci esset, praetermissa.

Example of a modern character portrayal in Livy's style.

De Alberto Einstein

Albertus Einstein inter naturae pervestigatores saeculi currentis longe procerrimus exsitit. Mundum enim universum necessitate mechanica, ut praecessores fecerant, describere noluit, sed ratione quodammodo fortuita eundem est contemplatus, qua demum nota nostrum saeculum praecipue imbuitur. Quam maxime a se dissentiebat, cum de operibus suis ad effectum photelectricum pertinentibus praemio ab illo Nobel vocato ornandus iam adulescens a schola propter examina pessime subita esset expulsus. Licet pacis auctor praesidi Civitatum Foederatarum Americae Septentrionalis Roosevelt litteras misit de periculo pyroboli atomici qui a Germanis praepararetur necnon de necessitate Americanorum his in rebus properandi, quo factum est ut pyrobolus atomicus Hirosimam Nagasakiumque deleturus apparatus sit conscientiae Alberti Einstein usque ad ultimum lumen obstrepiturus. De nodis totius mundi resolvendis meditabatur filio ipsius schizophrenia laborante tantum semel a patre adito omninoque neglecto ac derelicto. Fama est etiam Albertum Einstein, cui acroasis de rebus physicis esset habenda, omnibus auditoribus praestolantibus manu fidiculam seu violinam tenentem intravisse nulloque verbo prolato per duas horas opera illius Bach cecinisse, quippe qui in rhythmis musicis Bachianis eandem formulam mundi invenisse videretur, quae in perscrutationibus physicis esset quaerenda. Denique summa cum maestitia tum de tot hominibus in Iaponia innocentibus interfectis culpam sibi invehens tum de pervestigationibus postremis haud fructiferis dolens in nosocomio Principitoniensi haud gloriose princeps ingenii et doctrinae saeculi vicesimi mortem obivit.

3. Moral and philosophic treatises

In writing moral or philosophical texts, we may follow as an example
Cicero's treatises for their practical ideas and the hypotactic harmony
of their language; or Seneca whose philosophy is also a set of precepts
on how to live, but one that revolves around discovering ways of meeting
the challenges of life, and is presented in much easier paratactic rhythms.
Philosophical speculation should point to clear and explicit practical
conclusions. Latin cannot convey vague concepts.

Possible topics: *De amore et familia; Qui sit vitae humanae finis;
Quomodo animi tranquillitas obtineri liceat; De notitiae humanae
limitibus; Quid sit felicitas.*

Example from *Senecae Ad Lucilium I, 1*

*1. Ita fac, mi Lucili: vindica te tibi, et tempus quod adhuc aut
auferebatur aut subripiebatur aut excidebat collige et serva. Persuade
tibi hoc sic esse ut scribo: quaedam tempora eripiuntur nobis,
quaedam subducuntur, quaedam effluunt. Turpissima tamen est
iactura quae per neglegentiam fit. Et si volueris attendere, maxima
pars vitae elabitur male agentibus, magna nihil agentibus, tota vita
aliud agentibus. Quem mihi dabis qui aliquod pretium tempori ponat,
qui diem aestimet, qui intellegat se cottidie mori? In hoc enim fallimur,
quod mortem prospicimus: magna pars eius iam praeteriit; quidquid
aetatis retro est mors tenet. Fac ergo, mi Lucili, quod facere te scribis,
omnes horas complectere; sic fiet ut minus ex crastino pendeas, si
hodierno manum inieceris. Dum differtur vita transcurrit. Omnia,
Lucili, aliena sunt, tempus tantum nostrum est; in huius rei unius
fugacis ac lubricae possessionem natura nos misit, ex qua expellit
quicumque vult. Et tanta stultitia mortalium est ut quae minima et
vilissima sunt, certe reparabilia, imputari sibi cum impetravere
patiantur, nemo se iudicet quicquam debere qui tempus accepit, cum
interim hoc unum est quod ne gratus quidem potest reddere.*

Example of a modern composition on a philosophical topic in Seneca's style.

De taedio vitae fugando

Hodiernis temporibus multi taedio vitae vexantur. Cur vivant ignorant vel a vita desciscere volunt. Neminem cariorem habent nec quicquam dignum inveniunt quod finis fiat vitae vivendae. Ergo in diem vivunt vel voluptatibus pusillis traditi vel animo fracti. Eorum vita sensu carens dissipatur. Si tamen vita sine ratione esse videtur, rationem invenias oportet. Una tantum vita nobis est donata. Licet multis calamitatibus atque iniustitiis abundet, nos vero ipsi aliquid boni efficere possumus. Patientia ergo, amore et sedulitate oportet utaris. Porro qui dicunt vitam omnino iucunditate egere, perperam dicunt. Cogita de ortu et occasu solis quem cottidie admirari licet! Revoca in mentem risum infantuli integri qui aures animamque mulcet! Meditare de manibus amicorum inter se complexis! Quid autem de oblectamento operis perfecti et de gaudio amoris loquendum? Vita plena iucunditatis et laetitiae esse potest, vere vivenda, omnibus numeris digna.

4. Accusatory and defensive speeches

In writing accusatory or defensive speeches, we may follow mainly Cicero's speeches in their complex argumentation and the syntactic perfection of their expression. In these speeches, Cicero's language is similar to a perfect sphere since one cannot add or remove any part without disrupting the integrity of the whole.

In writing such speeches, we will need to work on the organization of the material *in utramque partem.*

Possible topics: defensive and accusatory speeches pro and con certain persons or certain virtues and vices.

Example from *Ciceronis In Catilinam, I, 5*

Quae cum ita sint, Catilina, perge quo coepisti: egredere aliquando ex urbe; patent portae; proficiscere! Nimium diu te imperatorem tua illa Manliana castra desiderant. Educ tecum etiam omnis tuos, si minus, quam plurimos; purga urbem. Magno me metu liberaveris, modo inter me atque te murus intersit. Nobiscum versari iam diutius non potes; non feram, non patiar, non sinam. Magna dis immortalibus habenda est atque huic ipsi Iovi Statori, antiquissimo custodi huius urbis, gratia, quod hanc tam taetram, tam horribilem tamque infestam rei publicae pestem totiens iam effugimus. Non est saepius in uno homine summa salus periclitanda rei publicae. Quam diu mihi consuli designato, Catilina, insidiatus es, non publico me praesidio, sed privata diligentia defendi. Cum proximis comitiis consularibus me consulem in campo et competitores tuos interficere voluisti, compressi conatus tuos nefarios amicorum praesidio et copiis nullo tumultu publice concitato; denique, quotienscumque me petisti, per me tibi obstiti, quamquam videbam perniciem meam cum magna calamitate rei publicae esse coniunctam. Nunc iam aperte rem publicam universam petis, templa deorum immortalium, tecta urbis, vitam omnium civium, Italiam totam ad exitium et vastitatem vocas.

Example of a modern accusatory speech in Cicero's style.

In amorem sui invectiva

Quid vosmetipsos amantes nonnisi in commodum vestrum incumbitis? Num homo a ceteris interclusus, tamquam si in deserto quodam aut in silva commoraretur, sibi tantum vivit? Nonne consociatio hominum atque communitas exstat, qua non solum fruimur lucrum percepturi, verum cui etiam ministros nos praebeamus oportet? Rettulerunt humani animi investigatores infantibus derelictis atque ab animalibus nutritis ingenium ad amorem sui minime esse proclive. Scimus autem Deo istum amorem sui esse alienum, quippe qui Filium unicum sacrificaverit stirpis humanae redemptorem. Solius ergo hominis vitium amoris sui abominabile proprium videtur, quo fit, ut ille ne bestiis quidem anteponatur. Si quis suis commodis consulit nec cuiquam, quae sua censet, dispertire vult, reminiscatur se nisi ab aliis adiutum eadem non fuisse adepturum. Petentes qui arcentur, cum primum opus fuerit, instanter vocantur ad adiutricem operam praestandam a quibus paulo ante erant reiecti. Nemo solus suis utatur, nam omnes alii ab aliis pendent. Itaque quo libentius proximis subveneris, eo felicius aliorum auxilio gaudebis.

5. Autobiographical pieces

In writing autobiographical accounts, we may follow Augustine for his poetic touch and the simplicity of language appropriate for such texts.

Example from *Augustini Confessiones, VIII, 12, 28-29*

XII. 28. Ubi vero a fundo arcano alta consideratio traxit et congessit totam miseriam meam in conspectu cordis mei, oborta est procella ingens ferens ingentem imbrem lacrimarum. Et ut totum effunderem cum vocibus suis, surrexi ab Alypio - solitudo mihi ad negotium flendi aptior suggerebatur - et secessi remotius, quam ut posset mihi onerosa esse etiam eius praesentia. Sic tunc eram, et ille sensit: nescio quid enim, puto, dixeram, in quo apparebat sonus vocis meae iam fletu gravidus, et sic surrexeram. Mansit ergo ille ubi sedebamus nimie stupens. Ego sub quadam fici arbore stravi me nescio quomodo et dimisi habenas lacrimis, et proruperunt flumina oculorum meorum, acceptabile sacrificium tuum, et non quidem his verbis, sed in hac sententia multa dixi tibi: Et tu, domine, usquequo? Usquequo, domine, irasceris in finem? Ne memor fueris iniquitatum nostrarum antiquarum. Sentiebam enim eis me teneri. Iactabam voces miserabiles: "Quamdiu, quamdiu 'cras et cras'? Quare non modo? Quare non hac hora finis turpitudinis meae?"

29. Dicebam haec et flebam amarissima contritione cordis mei. Et ecce audio vocem de vicina domo cum cantu dicentis et crebro repetentis quasi pueri an puellae, nescio: "Tolle lege, tolle lege". Statimque mutato vultu intentissimus cogitare coepi, utrumnam solerent pueri in aliquo genere ludendi cantitare tale aliquid, nec occurrebat omnino audisse me uspiam repressoque impetu lacrimarum surrexi nihil aliud interpretans divinitus mihi iuberi, nisi ut aperirem codicem et legerem quod primum caput invenissem.

Example of a modern composition of an autobiographical piece in Augustine's style.

De terrae tremore

Nocte illa bracchiis Morphei tenebar suavi devinctus sopore, cum terra ingenti mota est concussu. Lectulus enim meus vacillabat necnon stridor parietum audiebatur. Quid, Domine, fiebat? Quid mihi erat faciendum? Surrexi a lectulo, cucurri ad fenestram et, o spectaculum horrificum, aedes finitimae tamquam casurae titubabant. Rui ad scalas. In quinta contignatione manere plenum periculi videbatur. Tum autem nesciebam scalas periculosiores esse. Nec ceteri hoc scire videbantur. Nam magna turba hominum decurrebat aliis in alios irruentibus. Vagitus infantium, gemitus senum audiebatur. Deo gratias, tandem aliquando exire potui. Terra amplius non tremebat. Inspexi ad caelum. Luna nebulis abscondebatur et iterum illis motis apparebat. Ipse tremui cogitans quam caduca esset vita humana atque incerta. Paene totam noctem sub divo mansimus. Erant qui animo fracti domos suas redire nollent; alii vero spe quadam erecti terrae motum non repetitum iri iam Lares suos desiderabant. Primo diluculo in diaetam meam ascendi. Deo gratias egi quod omnia ita erant atque antea. In lectulo calido obdormivi.

6. Letters

A letter begins with the name of the writer in nominative, followed by the name of the addressee in dative, often accompanied by affectionate adjectives or appositives indicating titles. After the nominative and the dative, there follows one of these expressions: *s.d.* (=*salutem dicit*), *s.p.d.* (=*salutem plurimam dicit*) or only *s.* (=*salutem*).

Tullius Terentiae suae, Tulliolae suae, Ciceroni suo s.d.

The initial greeting formula is sometimes followed by *S.V.B.E.E.V.* (=*Si vales, bene est. Ego valeo.*), *S.V.B.E.E.Q.V.* (=*Si vales, bene est. Ego quoque valeo.*), or *S.V.B.E.V.* (=*Si vales, bene est. Valeo*). Military letters may begin with *S.T.E.Q.V.B.E.* (=*Si tu exercitusque valetis, bene est.*)

A letter concludes with final greetings: *vale; valete; cura ut valeas; fac valeas; si me amas, cura ut valeas; etiam atque etiam vale; valetudinem tuam cura diligenter; fac ut valetudinem tuam cures; da operam ut valeas; maximam da operam ut valeas, si me vis valere; valetudinem tuam fac ut cures; vale et mox mihi scribas seu potius scriptites.*

The address, either in the initial greeting or near the beginning of the letter (but not in the very beginning of the first sentence), may be accompanied by appositives expressing affection or respect: *meum corculum; meum cor; mi anime; mi animule; mi ocelle; mea lux; mea vita; deliciae meae; carissimae animae; desideria mea; suavissima et optatissima uxor; vir optime; spectatissime Domine; praestantissima Domina; iucundissima Dominula; Reverendissime Pater.* The addressee's name in the initial greeting may be accompanied by *suo, suae, suis* indicating friendship and respect without being too familiar.

At the end of the letter, the writer writes *dabam* (while *epistulam* as a direct object and *tabellario*, i.e., the courier, as an indirect object are implied) or *scribebam*, followed by the date (usually without the year), and then the name of the city as a location (in the locative or ablative) or as a departure (in the ablative). The formulae *dabam* and *scribebam* are in the imperfect as a courtesy for the addressee in putting the action in his temporal point of view.

In fact, we sometimes use in letters the imperfect or perfect to indicate an action that is taking place at the moment of writing; we use the pluperfect to indicate an action that has taken place before the moment of writing; and we use the periphrastic conjugation of the indicative imperfect (*-urus eram*) to indicate an action that would come after the moment of writing. We use adverbs of time in a similar way. Often in letters *hodie* becomes *eo die*, *heri* becomes *pridie*, *cras* becomes *postridie*.

Pridie aliam epistulam a te acceperam. (=Heri aliam epistulam a te accepi.)

Postridie de rebus eo die gestis te certiorem eram facturus. (= Cras de rebus hodie gestis te certiorem faciam.)

Most letters that have come to us from the classical period are by Cicero and Pliny the Younger. Seneca's letters have the literary form of a letter, but are in fact moral treatises.

Examples from *Plinii Epistulae I, XI* and *V, XVIII*.

C. Plinius Fabio Iusto suo s.

Olim mihi nullas epistulas mittis. Nihil est, inquis, quod scribam. At hoc ipsum scribe, nihil esse quod scribas, vel solum illud unde incipere priores solebant: "Si vales, bene est; ego valeo." Hoc mihi sufficit; est enim maximum. Ludere me putas? Serio peto. Fac sciam quid agas, quod sine sollicitudine summa nescire non possum. Vale.

C. Plinius Calpurnio Macro suo s.

Bene est mihi quia tibi bene est. Habes uxorem tecum, habes filium; frueris mari fontibus viridibus agro villa amoenissima. Neque enim dubito esse amoenissimam, in qua se composuerat homo felicior, ante quam felicissimus fieret. Ego in Tuscis et venor et studeo, quae interdum alternis, interdum simul facio; nec tamen adhuc possum pronuntiare, utrum sit difficilius capere aliquid an scribere. Vale.

Example of a modern composition of a letter.

Marcus patri suo et matri suae s.p.d.
Si valetis, bene est; ego valeo. Litteras vestras magno cum gaudio acceperam, pro quibus gratias maximas vobis ago. Veniam, quaeso, detis, quod tardius rescripsi quam debueram. Tempus enim mihi non suppeditaverat ut statim responderem. Nam cottidie mane scholas adeo, post meridiem et vesperi in linguam Latinam et Graecam incumbo. Roma est urbs pulcherrima, sed vix queo eam circumspicere. Quid aliud scribam? Permulta sunt, sed plura coram.
Haec in praesenti hactenus. Vobis tamen iterum scripturus eram de die adventus mei.
Meis verbis salutate, quaeso, avum et aviam meam. Curam diligenter detis ut valeatis. Iterum iterumque valete!
Scribebam Urbe Kalendis Martiis

Bibliography

Allcroft, A.H., A.J.F. Collins, *Higher Latin Composition*, London, University Tutorial Press 1911.

Arnold, T.K., G.G. Bradley, *A Practical Introduction to Latin Prose Composition*, London, Longmans 1934.

Bennett, Ch.E., *New Latin Composition*, Boston, Allyn and Bacon 1912 (reprinted Wauconda, Illinois, Bolchazy-Carducci 1996).

Bernini, E., *Latino vivente: avviamento allo scrivere latino*, Torino, S.E.I. 1942.

D'Arbela, E.V., *Avviamento al comporre latino*, Milano and Messina, Principato 1942.

Della Corte, F., *La composizione latina*, Torino, Silvio Gheroni editore 1951.

Gildersleeve, B.L., G. Lodge, *Latin Grammar*, Bristol, Bristol Classical Press 1895 (reprinted 1997).

Glücklich, H.-J., R. Nickel, P. Petersen, *Interpretatio: Neue Lateinische Textgrammatik*, Freiburg and Würzburg, Verlag Ploetz 1980.

Happ, H., *Grundfragen einer Dependenz-Grammatik der Lateinischen*, Göttingen, Vandenhoeck & Ruprecht 1976.

Landfester, M., *Einführung in die Stilistik der griechischen und lateinischen Literatursprachen*, Darmstadt, Wissenschaftliche Buchgesellschaft 1997.

Menge, H., *Lateinische Synonymik*, siebte, unveränderte Auflage von O. Schönberger, Heidelberg, Carl Winter 1988.

Menge, H., *Repertorium der lateinischen Syntax und Stilistik,* bearb. von A. Thierfelder, Darmstadt, Wissenschaftliche Buchgesellschaft 1979.

Mir, I.M., *Probata ratio scribendi et interpungendi in scriptis Latinis*, Romae, Academia Latinitati fovendae 1990.

Nägelsbach von, K. F., *Lateinische Stilistik für Deutsche*, Darmstadt, Wissenschaftliche Buchgesellschaft 1963.

Nairn, J.A., *Latin Prose Composition*, Cambridge, Cambridge University Press 1926.

North, M.A., A.E. Hillard, *Latin Prose Composition*, London, Duckworth 1993 (reprinted Wauconda, Illinois, Bolchazy-Carducci 1995).

Paoli, U.E., *Scrivere latino: guida a comporre e a tradurre in lingua latina*, Milano, Principato 1948.

Pekkanen, T., *Ars grammatica*, Helsinki, Gaudeamus 1982.

Pinkster H., *Latin Syntax and Semantics*, translated by H. Mulder, London and New York, Routledge 1990.

Scherer, A., *Handbuch der lateinischen Syntax*, Heidelberg, Carl Winter 1975.

Springhetti, A., *Exercitationes variae stili Latini, (=Latinitas perennis, III)*, Romae, Schola superior litterarum Latinarum in Pontificia Universitate Gregoriana 1956.

Springhetti, A., *Institutiones stili Latini, (=Latinitas perennis, II)*, Romae, Schola superior litterarum Latinarum in Pontificia Universitate Gregoriana 1954.

Traina, A., T. Bertotti, *Sintassi normativa della lingua latina*, vol. 1 Teoria, vol. 2 Esercizi, Bologna, Cappelli editore 1993.

Von Albrecht, M., *Masters of Roman Prose, From Cato to Apuleius. Interpretative Studies,* translated by N. Adkin, Leeds, Francis Cairns 1989.

Woodcock, E.C., *A New Latin Syntax*, Bristol and Oak Park, Bristol Classical Press and Bolchazy-Carducci Publishers 1959 (reprinted 1987).

Texts

Catulli Veronensis liber, ed. W. Eisenhut, Leipzig, Teubner 1983.

C. Plini Caecili Secundi Epistularum libri decem, recognovit brevique adnotatione critica instruxit R.A.B. Mynors, Oxonii, e typographeo Clarendoniano, 1963 (1966 reprinted with corrections).

L. Annaei Senecae Dialogorum libri duodecim, recognovit brevique adnotatione critica instruxit L.D. Reynolds, Oxonii, e typographeo Clarendoniano 1977.

Lucius Annaeus Seneca, Ad Lucilium, epistulae morales, recognovit et adnotatione critica instruxit L.D. Reynolds, tomus I, libri I-XIII, Oxonii, e typographeo Clarendoniano 1965.

M. Tulli Ciceronis Epistulae ad familiares: Libri I-XVI, ed. D.R. Shackleton Bailey, Stutgardiae, Teubner 1988.

M. Tulli Ciceronis Orationes, tomus I, ed. A.C. Clark, Oxonii, e typographeo Clarendoniano 1961.

M. Tulli Ciceronis Orationes, tomus III, ed. G. Peterson, Oxonii, e typographeo Clarendoniano s.a. (1917, editio altera recognita et emendata).

M. Val. Martialis Epigrammata, ed. W.M. Lindsay, Oxonii, e typographeo Clarendoniano 1977 (editio altera).

S. Aureli Augustini Confessionum libri XIII, ed. M. Skutella, ed. corr. cur. H. Jürgens et W. Schaub, Stutgardiae et Lipsiae, Teubner 1996.

Tacite, Annales (livres XIII-XVI), texte établi et traduit par P. Wuilleumier, Paris, Les belles lettres 1978.

Titi Livi Ab Urbe condita, libri XXI-XXII, recognovit Th. A. Dorey, Lipsiae, Teubner 1971.